WHY SHRINK- WRAP A CUCUMBER?

ISBN:
978-1-
85669-
7576

9 781856 697576

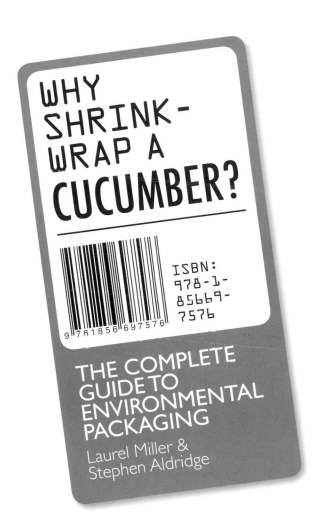

WHY SHRINK-WRAP A CUCUMBER?

ISBN: 978-1-85669-7576

9 781856 697576

THE COMPLETE GUIDE TO ENVIRONMENTAL PACKAGING

Laurel Miller & Stephen Aldridge

LAURENCE KING PUBLISHING

LAURENCE KING

Published in 2012 by
Laurence King Publishing Ltd
361–373 City Road
London EC1V 1LR
Tel: +44 20 7841 6900
Fax: +44 20 7841 6910
email: enquiries@laurenceking.com
www.laurenceking.com

A catalogue record for this book is available from the British Library.

ISBN 13: 978 1 85669 757 6

Design: TwoSheds Design

Printed in China

INTRODUCTION

We are right to be preoccupied with wasteful packaging, but too many of us see all packaging as waste.

And why not? We did not want to buy the packaging. We wanted the product it contained, yet we are left with the task of disposing of the useless wrapper or container. And what happens to the wrapper or container? More often than not, it is thrown into a bin with all the other packaging, and is eventually dumped in a hole in the ground with millions more wrappers and containers.

Packaging has to a large extent helped shape the world in which we live. It enables us to pursue a lifestyle rich in convenience and choice that allows us to enjoy, for relatively little cost, high-quality goods from across the globe, safe in the knowledge that they will be fresh, undamaged and uncontaminated.

But convenience comes at a price. Packaging has come to be seen as the epitome of wastefulness and excess, yet in reality it is the only visible remnant of a string of energy- and resource-hungry processes that contribute to creating the goods we buy. When we purchase a product we do not think about the raw materials, irrigation, energy, fuel and pollution in its wake. We simply see the product, which we make use of, and its packaging, which we throw away, so it is no surprise that packaging has become the focus for concern about the environment.

How packaging is disposed of is understandably seen as an area where households can make an active contribution to the environment on a personal level – nowhere more so than around the weekly food shop, where most of a family's waste is generated. In a system where the amount of waste we get rid of is increasingly limited by the number of rubbish bags allowed per household, as well as biweekly collections and even weight restrictions, the emphasis is increasingly on recycling. This makes recycling collections popular for both their environmental feel-good factor and the pure practicality of being able to dispose of a certain proportion of the packaging waste generated during the course of a week.

Beneficial though it may be, the recycling process encourages us to be unfairly judgemental. Good

Supermarket shopping

packaging goes in the recycling bin, bad packaging into the waste bin. Despite our desire to protect the planet, the most environmentally friendly course is often not clear, either to the consumer or to the people who design and specify packaging.

Even the terminology associated with the environment can be vague or open to interpretation.

Green is in one sense simply another word for sustainable, but in the political arena (and it is a political word) it extends to global environmental protection, support for a low-carbon economy and social responsibility. The global village is a well-worn metaphor for the ease with which we can trade, travel and communicate throughout the world, and awareness of our status as a global community has led to a growing perception that we are all responsible for protecting the planet. Paradoxically,

Clockwise from above:
Prepacked vegetables

Fresh flowers delivered from Kenya

A typical production line for FMCG

Conveyor belt used in coal mining

many people believe that one of the ways to do this is to focus more keenly on our local areas. Bioregionalism, as this is called, promotes local trading and agriculture above sourcing goods from the other side of the world and is a key area in green philosophy.

Sustainability, in the context of the environment, is the ability to replace the resources used in a product's manufacture, and so ultimately make a neutral or positive contribution to the environment.

When allowance is made for the amount of additional energy use a material acquires during its production, harvesting, conversion and transportation, creating truly sustainable packaging is not a realistic goal, so the term has inaccurately become a catch-all description for anything that reduces the use of materials, including recycling and lightweighting.

Environmentally friendly is far less specific. It covers more or less any approach that results in reduced consumption of materials, or lower carbon dioxide emissions, but can also touch on other environmental factors, such as promoting biodiversity or protecting water sources. In most cases the more accurate term might be 'less environmentally damaging'.

Neither sustainable or environmentally friendly necessarily mean ethical. Many people who buy Fairtrade goods and avoid genetically modified products might be

extremely concerned at some of the practices used to help save the planet. The market for environmentally friendly materials is just that – a market, with many products competing on performance and price. Some of the materials are questionable, both in terms of ethics and environmental benefit. For example, they can contribute to the destruction of rainforests or ancient woodland by increasing the demand for farmland. Other examples are the use of genetically modified crops, the diversion of farmland to non-food production (causing food shortages), the reduction of biodiversity, bonded labour, poor and unsafe working conditions for workers who recycle waste, and widespread contamination from unregulated recycling practices. Surprisingly, some environmental organizations are quick to support so-called 'sustainable' materials without really considering the damage they can cause.

MAKING PROGRESS

The planet's resources are not unlimited, and despite its astonishing ability to absorb the impact of the excesses of industrialization and consumerism, it is increasingly clear that things will have to change.

Packaging has not yet achieved anything like its potential to reduce its impact on the environment, but, as is befitting in a convenience society, it is a convenient high-visibility target that deflects attention from less palatable forms of environmental action, such as reducing our dependence on high-carbon fossil fuels and heavy industry. Its branding power is unquestionable, and it can also be functional, protective, informative, creative, even witty. It is certainly no stranger to controversy. People's concern is now keenly and rightly focused on protecting the environment, but in the past other issues, like food safety, contamination, security, even openability, have been routine public preoccupations that frequently made headlines in the national press.

Designers and specifiers do not go out of their way to create waste, but they have to make realistic decisions about product protection, cost, transportation and merchandising, and often have to work within existing packaging systems. There are undoubtedly some retailers and manufacturers who choose to create an impression of value or quality by using oversized, unnecessary or intricate packaging, but by and large these are a shrinking minority. Nevertheless, certain retail sectors are significantly more prone to using wasteful packaging than others and improvements can be made across the board.

Most manufacturers are happy to cut back their packaging, where possible, if only to reduce costs. In some cases, such as Easter egg packaging in the United Kingdom, environmental pressures from government and public alike have in effect given them permission to suspend mutual competition in manufacturing overpresented products, and return to saner levels of packaging and more realistic manufacturing costs.

Government and consumer pressure have created a situation where manufacturers and retailers want, and need, to achieve smaller environmental footprints while presenting their products in the best possible light. For packaging designers and specifiers this is every bit as much an opportunity as it is a challenge. True, there are many restrictions, but the growing realization that we need to rethink our priorities has led to a huge amount of exciting activity, with different approaches to design, a bewildering array of new materials and a massive reservoir of positive intention from manufacturers.

In tapping all this unexplored potential it is important that, as designers and specifiers, we pursue genuinely beneficial (or less damaging) packaging solutions, are not taken in by some of the more dubious, yet plausible claims of materials manufacturers and do not court the consumer with green window-dressing.

In this book we aim to steer a path through the environmental maze, to ensure that good packaging design is also good for the environment. We will explore the issues behind environmentally friendly packaging, how

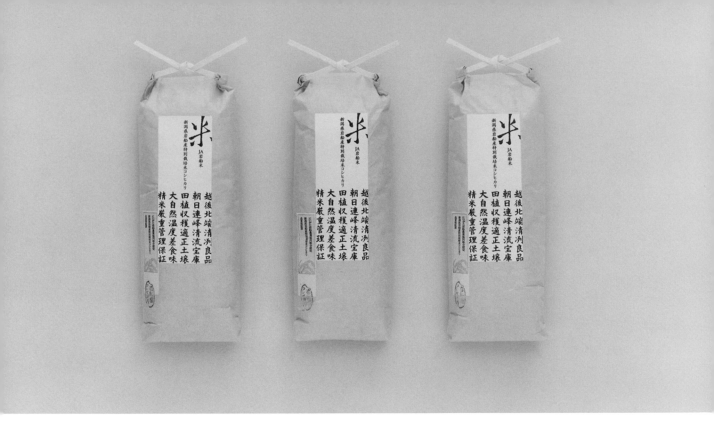

consumers relate to it and how designers can make informed choices about design and materials. This is a fast-moving field, progressing all the time, so being able to evaluate new developments effectively as they are introduced is as important as keeping up to date with the current crop.

We simply do not accept that for a pack to be eco-friendly it must be stripped of all its personality and substance. There are many different ways of approaching environmental packaging without being sucked into a brave new world of unbleached paper and pulp. Neither do we want to preach; any packaging reduction is better than none at all. It can be damaging to a brand to reduce its packaging to the barest minimum and this is not always the best way to help the environment. So, this is certainly not a 'how to do it' book of design, but we hope it will give you both the information and some of the inspiration to make a difference without compromising on creativity.

Above:
Designed by Kenya Hara, Iwafune rice packaging is honest and beautiful

Right:
Designed by Big Fish, Dorset cereals reveals the product through a stamped-out design

CHAPTER 1

PACKAGING AND THE ENVIRONMENT

PACKAGING IS A REFLECTION OF OUR CONSUMER SOCIETY AND TO A LARGE EXTENT IT HAS HELPED SHAPE THE WORLD WE LIVE IN. IT HELPS US TRANSPORT VAST QUANTITIES OF GOODS FROM CONTINENT TO CONTINENT AND TOWN TO TOWN. IT PRESERVES AND PROTECTS OUR FOOD FROM CONTAMINATION. IT ALLOWS US TO INHABIT THE CONVENIENCE CULTURE, WHICH PERVADES EVERY ASPECT OF MODERN LIFE. IT ADDS VALUE AND TEXTURE TO THE PRODUCTS WE BUY.

IN THIS CHAPTER WE EXPLORE THE USE AND ABUSE OF PACKAGING, AND LOOK AT WHY IT HAS BECOME LINKED TO THE DISCUSSION OF GLOBAL WARMING AND WHETHER ITS LABEL AS THE VILLAIN IS JUSTIFIED.

WHAT IS PACKAGING
AND WHY DO WE NEED IT?

THE RISE OF THE CONVENIENCE CULTURE

In the early part of the twentieth century convenience food amounted to canned and dried/powdered goods, but innovations in preparation, packaging, transportation and merchandising led to fresher, tastier and, in many cases, healthier foods. Frozen foods on an industrial scale were made practical by Clarence Birdseye, who developed his fast-freezing technique in the 1920s. After initial reluctance from retailers to invest in freezer cabinets, frozen food proved its worth during the Second World War (when steel for cans was in short supply) and became commonplace in the 1950s. With the widespread adoption of chiller cabinets and improvements in the supply chain in the 1960s, as well as the availability of cheaper domestic freezers, the possibilities for selling fresh and frozen prepared foods mushroomed.

The post-war convenience-food revolution was inextricably linked to the march of progress by advertisers, contributing as it did to freedom from traditional domestic drudgery. It took place in an era of consumption and optimism, after the bleak austerity of the years immediately following the war. By the 1960s disposability was, more often than not, applauded, rather than questioned.

Supermarkets grew and grew, gradually displacing many traditional high-street shops. The butcher, baker, fishmonger, delicatessen largely succumbed to their dominance. Personal service and quality soon became subordinate to convenience and modernity. The resulting shift from buying ingredients and whole produce to buying prepared foods, both precooked and raw, means there are now limited alternatives to supermarket shopping. So much food is prepacked and prepared that a significant number of people never cook with fresh ingredients.

Today, as well as convenience, supermarkets offer access to exotic dishes from around the world, using globally sourced ingredients. Few of us make our own fresh pasta or even soup. Many busy people are unwilling to spend time shopping for ingredients and preparing food when a freshly made packaged version is already on the shelves. And, for those who prefer to cook their own

Above:
Preprepared and ready-to-use foods

Below:
Out-of-town filling station and the interior of a 24-hour convenience store

food, supermarkets offer prepackaged cuts of meat, prepared salads and shrink-wrapped vegetables.

Not very many years ago eyebrows would have been raised at the sight of baking potatoes individually labelled and shrink-wrapped on to a tray, whether the tray was made of recycled paper pulp or plastic. Now, despite the growth in environmental awareness, it is not unusual to see all kinds of fruit and vegetables, including ones that are perfectly able to look after themselves, packed this way.

In effect, the convenience culture and the way we choose to buy food are bound to generate a high demand for packaging. People like the idea of shopping at the local butcher, baker or greengrocer, or at farmers' markets, but in reality supermarkets have more power than ever, with their massive choice of products, low prices and convenient opening hours. Originally dominant in the high street and out-of-town retail parks, smaller supermarkets are now squeezing the local businesses on their doorsteps. They are so ubiquitous that no visit to a filling station or motorway services is complete without an opportunity to buy groceries from one or other retail chain. Even with the will to seek out fresher produce with less packaging, most people simply do not have the time to visit several shops. Why would they when everything they need can be purchased under one roof? It might even be argued that, despite generating more packaging waste, a single visit to the supermarket is less harmful to the environment than making several car journeys to do the weekly shopping.

THE POSITIVES OF PACKAGING

Retailers and manufacturers have many reasons to like packaging and the first is **physical protection**. For instance, soft fruit is usually sold in plastic punnets to reduce bruising, electronic goods have a degree of cushioning and meringues are often sold in plastic clam packs, all of which could be seen as overpackaging. Packaging also protects the product from **tampering**, high-profile examples of which can include criminal attempts to interfere with foods. Realistically, most tampering is done either with the aim of stealing the product or, more likely, simply to inspect it. Goods are often sealed in welded clam packs (see p. 220). Although this is a particularly wasteful pack format, not only does it prevent tampering and contamination, it usually displays the product clearly, allowing a good area for promotional graphics, and also has the potential for sculpted shapes, which can help enhance a brand. It is very common to see clam packs that bear no relation to the size of product they contain. Some retailers prefer large packs that help to prevent **pilfering**, because it is more difficult to hide them in clothing.

Packaging can extend the **shelf life** of perishable produce as it not only limits contact with the atmosphere, but also offers the possibility of using inert gases or heat treatment to delay the onset of decay without using additives. Extended shelf life is a huge benefit to retailers as it helps reduce the cost of turning over stock, reduces waste and limits the need to mark down prices of expired goods. Cuts of meat are shrink-wrapped on to plastic trays, usually with an absorbent pad to soak up any excess blood, and last much longer in the gas-flushed modified-atmosphere packaging (see p. 218), which protects them from airborne bacteria. Good packaging also gives even unattractive products, including those cuts of meat, **visual appeal**. For instance, meat in a limp plastic bag, purchased from a butcher, does not look good and nor do cereals bagged loose in a whole-food store. The appeal, in these cases, is based almost entirely on perceived product quality.

Apart from the need for basic **product information**, laws worldwide require an ever-increasing amount of statutory information – ingredients, safety or dietary advice, age restrictions, etc. – so finding the right balance between product marketing and obligatory legal text can be challenging. Packaging is the retailer/manufacturer's ideal vehicle for this information. In the case of fresh foods, this can mean the addition of a cardboard wrap (or carton) simply to carry information. Recently, efforts have increasingly been made to find ways of printing directly on to sealing film in order to do away with cartons and wraps.

The convenience culture is typified by kids' lunch products

Handling products effectively in the supply chain and in-store is another important aspect of retailing. For instance, most retailers require products to be easily arranged by staff in front-facing rows, and therefore prefer them to be either hangable or stackable (preferably both). They also often have strict rules governing pack height and depth, to which manufacturers must adhere if they want their products stocked. In addition, retailers frequently have detailed requirements concerning the sizes of outer cartons for palletization and handling.

WHEN CONVENIENCE TRUMPS NECESSITY

In their search for convenience and in pursuit of market share, supermarkets generate new product variants, which inevitably lead to pack formats that might otherwise be unnecessary. Butter, a perfectly manageable commodity when packed in a simple paper wrap, is now often packed in vacuum-formed plastic with a foil seal and plastic lid. This is to create not a superior-tasting product, but a more convenient one, which 'spreads straight from the fridge'. The market for supermarket sandwiches is in a similar vein. Before the 1980s it was normal to make sandwiches at home and take them to work in a lunch box, but as

sandwich shops exploiting the lunchtime snack market started to proliferate retailers saw an opportunity. Now sandwiches are a key part of many food retailers' late-morning sales. They are chilled, so stay fresh, and customers can choose from a wide range of fillings instead of making sandwiches hours earlier with leftovers from the fridge. So there is profit for the retailer, and choice and convenience for the customer.

However, each convenience innovation brings more packaging and sandwiches, because of their success, bring more than most. With worker's lunchtimes catered for by retailers and takeaway food outlets, the lunch box is now mainly relegated to schoolchildren. From the 1950s it was targeted by the producers of convenience prepacked mini cheeses. By the 1990s prepackaged crackers with ready-cut slices of cheese and ham had been launched. Today, supermarkets offer a wide range of lunch box-themed multipack snacks for children, from cereal snack bars and juice cartons to mini pull-top bottles. Few are intended for reuse.

Bottled water

BOTTLED WATER

Bottled waters are a newly revitalized and vastly profitable product sector. They came about through necessity as, for centuries, springs were among the few reliably pure sources of water – Perrier was first bottled in 1863 by decree of Napoleon III 'for the good of France' – and were essential for many years because piped water was not always potable. Although the quality of piped water improved, bottled water remained popular in many European countries and Perrier, in particular, with the aid of imaginative advertising campaigns, became fashionable worldwide. The manufacturers of bottled water exploited health and exercise trends as well as the club scene in the 1990s (remember Acid House?), and bottled water made the leap to being cool. Before long it was essential to stay hydrated on the move. The use of relatively cheap, lightweight PET (polyethylene terephthalate) bottles instead of glass ones made this more practical. The innovations continued, and today it is not unusual to see a PET bottle with a two-part screw-top that includes a pull-out 'sport' spout and a plastic overcap – for water. This uses a grotesque amount of plastic in the name of 'convenience' to do the extremely simple job of sealing the bottle.

Clearly the best packaging is no packaging. Less is more. However, few products can be sold unpackaged in the modern retail environment. So, if packaging has such a beneficial effect, why has it become such a pariah?

Several good reasons spring to mind, such as: wasting resources, overburdening landfills, harm to marine life, pollution of waterways and general littering of streets. Chiefly though, packaging is linked, by government agencies, environmental groups and consumers alike, to the process of global warming. Before we can begin to understand why – and whether it is justified – perhaps we should look at global warming itself.

GLOBAL WARMING

IT IS ALMOST UNIVERSALLY ACCEPTED THAT CLIMATE CHANGE IS HAPPENING AND THAT IT IS HAPPENING AS A RESULT OF HUMAN ACTIVITY. MOST PEOPLE ARE FAMILIAR WITH THE POTENTIAL EFFECTS OF GREENHOUSE GASES, SUCH AS CARBON DIOXIDE, METHANE AND NITROUS OXIDE, WHICH TRAP THE SUN'S RAYS WITH THE RESULT THAT THE EARTH GRADUALLY HEATS UP.

Over the last 200 years, since the start of the Industrial Revolution, these gases have been building up in the atmosphere at an ever-increasing rate, with the ultimate consequence that if temperatures rise high enough to melt the ice caps at the North and South Poles the amount of water released would significantly raise the level of the oceans, swamping low-lying land, destroying ecosystems and displacing populations on a massive scale, with all too imaginable consequences.

A sobering example of the current level of global warming can be found in an icebound Arctic stretch of ocean to the north of Russia. Over the centuries many explorers have searched in vain for a direct trade route by sea from Europe to Asia through the North-east Passage, but recently, because of global warming, it has become navigable for the first time in 5,000 years. This is excellent news for owners of cargo ships, as this route saves some 4,800 kilometres (3,000 miles) by avoiding the Suez Canal, but it is indicative of the extent to which the climate has already changed. Rising sea levels are also prompting the government of the low-lying Maldive islands, most of which are no higher than 1.5 metres (5 feet), to actively seek a new homeland, because they are faced with the harsh reality of inexorably rising sea levels.

Increased sea levels may be only a short-term effect of global warming. Some climatologists argue that the large quantities of fresh water released from melting ice caps could turn off the Gulf Stream, which takes warm currents to northern Europe and returns cooler water to the Caribbean in a hitherto perpetual cycle. This could ultimately, perhaps rapidly, cause a new ice age in the northern hemisphere.

THE CARBON CYCLE

Carbon dioxide (CO_2) is present in all life forms. It circulates in a process called the carbon cycle, where carbon in the atmosphere is absorbed by plants and photosynthesized into carbohydrates. When plants die they decay, releasing carbon back into the atmosphere or, if no oxygen is present, they release methane, another greenhouse gas. Carbon can also be released by combustion and volcanic eruptions, but some enters the soil (through dead plants and animals covered by sediment, for example) and over a process of millions of years it is compressed into coal or oil – the fossil fuels that are at the very heart of our energy technology.

When carbon is released by burning wood and other plant life the process is often said to be carbon neutral, as the carbon would have returned to the atmosphere

The carbon cycle

Above: **Forest plants seem to grow faster when carbon levels rise**

Opposite: **Wetlands are a prime source of natural methane**

anyway if the wood were allowed to decay. Animals absorb carbon by eating plants and other animals, and release it through respiration and decomposition. Carbon from the atmosphere dissolves readily into the oceans, where it takes the form of calcium carbonate in shells, plankton skeletons and coral.

The huge imbalance that causes carbon to build up in the atmosphere is a result of carbon, stored as fossil fuels, being suddenly (in geological terms) released into the atmosphere. This type of pollution from industry, cities and transportation systems has built up to an unsustainable degree. Currently, a great deal of the excess is soaked up by the oceans, which contain about 50 times more carbon than the atmosphere, but they cannot continue to absorb carbon at this rate for ever.

While scientists almost universally recognize that global warming is taking place as a result of human activity, some note a few anomalies. Recent evidence suggests that plants absorb more carbon in hazy polluted conditions, which may be because they absorb light more efficiently in diffused lighting conditions where there are fewer strong shadows. Scientists are also studying why forests seem to grow faster when carbon levels rise, but none of them suggest that plants can absorb carbon at anything like the rate at which we can produce it.

METHANE

Methane (CH_4) is about 23 times more potent as a greenhouse gas than carbon dioxide, but, whereas the latter can stay in the atmosphere for 50 to 100 years, methane remains there for approximately ten years. In nature it is emitted when plant-based materials break down anaerobically (in the absence of oxygen). The prime sources of this natural methane are wetlands, where dying plant and animal life becomes anaerobically sealed by the mixture of water and soil during the decaying process. However, the primary sources of man-made methane are landfill sites for waste disposal, where it is emitted by any material derived from plants or animals, including food

waste, paper, card, moulded pulp and bioplastics. The United States Greenhouse Gas Inventory of 2005 cites landfill methane as the highest single source of man-made methane; it claims that in 2003 it was the source of 34 per cent of methane in the atmosphere, slightly higher than emissions from natural sources. However, according to an Intergovernmental Panel on Climate Change (IPCC) report, by far the major sources of man-made methane are energy production and farm animals (ruminants, such as cows and sheep), with ruminants contributing 4.5 per cent more emissions than energy production. The IPCC also found that these two emissions were roughly equivalent to natural emissions of methane – although total man-made emissions exceed natural emissions by 20 per cent. Methane's imminent threat in the global-warming process is that if the ice caps melt, methane stored in the permafrost for thousands of years would be released into the atmosphere, greatly accelerating the global-warming process. However, the most recent research has shown that, after climbing for over a century, methane levels in the atmosphere are showing signs of levelling off.

NITROUS OXIDE

Nitrous oxide (N_2O) is 300 times more potent as a greenhouse gas than carbon dioxide. It is released when synthetic nitrate fertilizers are used in farming. Not only do the fertilizers emit the gas, but nitrates can leach into run-offs and streams, and indirectly release nitrous oxide as soon as the water is exposed to air. This may be linked to agriculture-based packaging, including pulp for paper and card that is often intensively grown in monoculture plantations, and bioplastics which are made from crops.

Nitrous oxide is also used as a propellant for food-related aerosols, such as those used for whipped cream and cooking oil. Although this usage is significant within the aerosol industry, it barely registers when compared to emissions from agriculture.

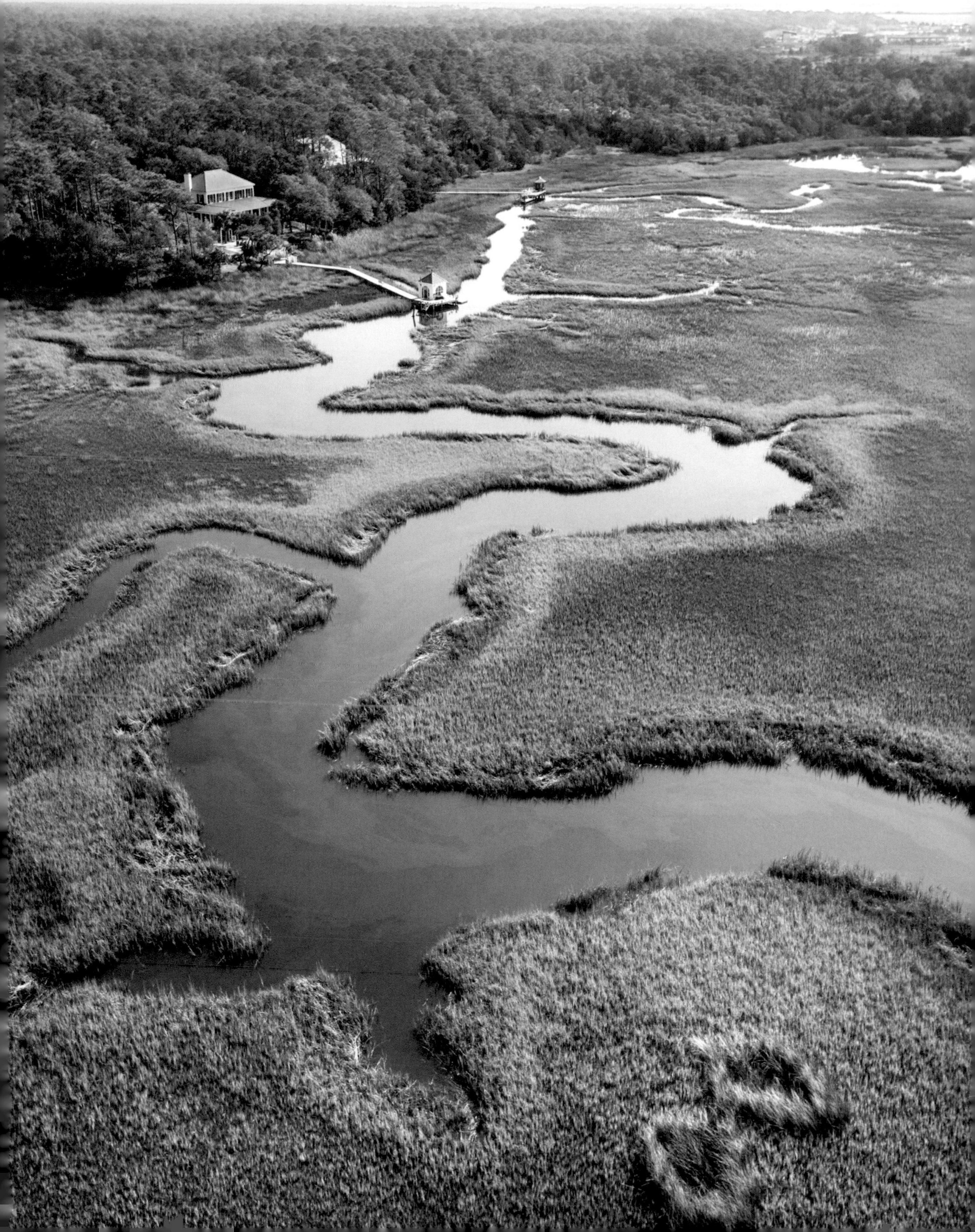

MAN AS CONSUMER
AND GLOBAL WARMING

ALL THE EVIDENCE POINTS
TOWARDS HUMAN ACTIVITY
AS THE PRIMARY CAUSE OF
GLOBAL WARMING, YET WE
CONTINUE TO OVERPRODUCE
AND WASTE OUR EVER MORE
PRECIOUS GLOBAL RESOURCES.
WE ALL CONSUME VASTLY
MORE THAN WE DID JUST
20 YEARS AGO. AS DEVELOPING
COUNTRIES LIKE CHINA AND
INDIA GROW WEALTHIER,
MORE PRESSURE IS PUT ON
DIMINISHING FOOD AND
ENERGY RESOURCES.

Above:
Supermarkets offer a huge choice

Above right:
Chinese workers on a production line

Below:
Container ships bringing goods produced in China

People in developing nations expect to live in air-conditioned comfort and have access to domestic appliances and electronic goods, such as hi-fis, computers and DVD players. They also expect to eat meat more regularly, but the price for this is increased use of energy and less efficient use of land: instead of crops being grown for food they are grown to feed cattle, which often leads to the destruction of forests to create more farmland.

The developed world has come to rely on cheap imports from the less developed world. Not only consumer goods, such as electrical appliances, clothing, electronic goods and toys, but also food. For people living in the West, choice has become their birthright, to the extent that it is not unusual to source foods from the other side of the world, to enjoy year-round availability of traditional produce and to experience new varieties of fruit and vegetables. Growing prosperity has raised expectations. The widespread use of chiller cabinets and modified-atmosphere packaging has made fresh foods look better and last longer. Air freight ensures that produce with a short life reaches the shelves more quickly. Produce or products from abroad are unlikely to be rejected by consumers on grounds other than cost or political sensitivity. For instance, some people might actively reject oranges from Israel (because they sympathize with the Palestinians) or, in the United Kingdom, apples from France (to support British farmers), but they tend not to question how much energy has been expended in bringing a product to the supermarket shelf from another continent.

WHY HAS PACKAGING BECOME LINKED WITH GLOBAL WARMING?

PACKAGING, AS IS BEFITTING IN A CONVENIENCE SOCIETY, IS A CONVENIENT HIGH-VISIBILITY TARGET: IT DEFLECTS ATTENTION FROM LESS PALATABLE FORMS OF ENVIRONMENTAL ACTION, SUCH AS REDUCING DEPENDENCE ON CARS, CONSUMER GOODS, HEAVY INDUSTRY, CENTRAL HEATING AND AIR CONDITIONING.

Softwood forests are often managed and farmed

In the context of the debate about global warming, and the human contribution towards it, it has become a symbol of wastefulness. Not without good reason. Packaging involves the production, conversion, transportation and disposal of vast quantities of materials such as card and paper, plastics, glass, aluminium and steel. At each stage of their journey, from cradle to grave, greenhouse gases are created.

Any process that involves the use of fossil-based fuels will emit carbon dioxide. Landfill sites, where much packaging ends its journey, are a major contributor to rising levels of methane from the anaerobic decomposition of plant-based materials. Nitrous oxide is specifically (but not exclusively) relevant to packaging because intensively farmed maize and sugar cane are used to make the biofuel ethanol and its bioplastic and pulp by-products, which are now becoming extremely sought after for use as 'environmentally friendly' packaging. Paper, too, is often grown in intensively farmed plantations.

IS PACKAGING REALLY THE VILLAIN?

Packaging undoubtedly plays a significant role in global warming, but perhaps not always to the extent that some would like to believe. For instance, although paper and card production undeniably affects old-growth forests, it also stimulates forestry, particularly in Europe. On the other hand, the actual process of producing paper can be extremely polluting, and, because paper is a plant-based product, if landfilled it will emit methane as it breaks down.

Plastics contribute to carbon emissions, but are largely a by-product of fuel production – accounting for only 4 per cent of oil extraction – which might otherwise be flared off straight into the atmosphere. Although a great deal of energy is used in their production, and they can create harmful emissions at this stage, they are a lightweight energy-saving alternative to other materials, and often have the potential to be recycled or reused. Fossil plastics are ultimately unsustainable, and will perhaps run out within 150 years, but they take up to

500 years to decompose so, given that carbon dioxide has a half-life in the atmosphere of 50–200 years, the likelihood that their embodied carbon would have a major effect on global warming is small, unlike emissions from fuel that are released into the atmosphere very quickly.

The production processes for glass, aluminium and steel are highly energy-intensive. However, recent developments in recycling have been extremely important in improving their environmental profile, particularly in the case of aluminium: only 5 per cent of the energy required to create aluminium from scratch is used to recycle it.

In the recent past packaging has in many ways been a victim of its own success. It is a great facilitator: it preserves and protects products, allows them to be moved cheaply and efficiently, reduces wastage and helps to increase speed of delivery. It could be argued that this enabling quality has more effect on the environment than the materials themselves, as it contributes to an energy-hungry global trading village unfettered by many of the limitations of the past. While few people would want to sacrifice any of the advantages packaging brings, the reality is that it uses energy and resources. The difference between the energy and resources used to prepare, transport, chill and display a product and those used to pack it is that the pack is physical and comes home with the customer, only to be discarded as soon as the product is used. It is the tangible evidence of our contribution to global warming. Having become the villain of the piece it is now imperative that packaging plays a high-profile role in helping to preserve the environment.

Five or ten years ago the packaging industry focused almost exclusively on innovation, hygiene and efficiency. However, retailers and manufacturers have not only acknowledged the need to address the effect packaging has on the planet, they have also realized that there is a great deal of money to be made by being seen to be green (or a great deal to be lost by missing the boat), so the emphasis has clearly shifted to sustainability and the environment.

HOW RETAILERS, CONSUMERS AND LEGISLATORS ARE BEGINNING TO EMBRACE ENVIRONMENTAL INITIATIVES

WE ARE AT THE START OF ADOPTING A GLOBALLY SUSTAINABLE APPROACH TO LIVING. MUCH IS STILL TO BE DONE, BUT AT LEAST WE RECOGNIZE MANY OF THE ISSUES. ADVANCES MAY COME WITH NEW TECHNOLOGY, MATERIALS, GREENER RETAILING, DEVELOPMENTS IN RECYCLING, LEGISLATION OR EVEN CONSUMER ATTITUDES.

Waitrose
Outdoor Living

cheers
4 champagne flutes

To a large extent, therefore, the ability to effect change will depend on the viewpoint of the three key players: the retailers and manufacturers, the consumers and the legislators.

RETAILERS AND MANUFACTURERS

Mass retailers, particularly supermarkets, often work to very small profit margins. They have to balance the consumer's expectations of product quality against their costs, while complying with stringent packaging and hygiene regulations. Retailers also have to ensure that the products they sell are safe, attractive, well-protected and good value, so for some of them 'eco-friendly' is towards the bottom of the list. However, some enterprising retailers have turned customers' concerns about the environment to their advantage by visibly focusing on improving their environmental profiles. Others have made only a few token gestures, such as charging for carrier bags. Making improvements to benefit the environment can be costly, and inevitably eats into profit margins, so an all-out environmental commitment has to be carefully considered against the potential reward. For instance, own-brand packaging lines may need to be changed to accommodate different materials. Materials such as recycled PET or card may be more expensive than standard ones and new pack formats may result in higher transport costs.

Times of economic turmoil, when margins are squeezed and consumers have less to spend, are a true test of the environmental resolve of both retailers and their customers. In supermarket retailing the premium chains that focus on quality are often the most proactive in protecting the environment, because the additional cost of eco-friendly packaging is more easily absorbed into their overall costs, and is favourably offset by increasing their green credentials in the eyes of customers. Budget chains, with their 'pile it high, sell it low' approach, tend to be less proactive, as their customers are seen as being primarily concerned with value for money, although the stores usually make some sort of high-profile green gesture.

For manufacturers, packaging is a necessary evil. Most tend to see it as an unwanted additional cost that cuts into their profit margins, but recognize its importance in protecting and promoting their products. So their attitudes to it are broadly similar to those of retailers. Packaging allows them to bring a product safely to the consumer, and often prolongs its unpackaged shelf life, so the pack format (for example, a bottle, can, carton, etc.) can be as critical as the cost. Manufacturers do not welcome burdensome additional regulation from the state, but many recognize the need for green initiatives and are happy to be seen to be green if this does not eat into their margins. Some of them have turned environmental concerns to their advantage; one way is to market concentrated versions of products, which reduces pack materials, saves energy in transportation and makes a genuine contribution to the environment. Detergent manufacturers have been particularly proactive in this respect by producing not only concentrated products but also ones that save energy by working at lower temperatures. A wide range of liquid products could theoretically benefit from this approach; concentrated versions of some fresh soups or 'fresh' fruit juices are examples.

Broadening the sustainable approach

In the past, green retailing was to some extent aimed at the affluent, liberal middle class and often smacked of tokenism – a few high-visibility pulp cases or brown boxes printed in one colour swimming in a sea of otherwise plastic packaging – but it is surprising how quickly a more sustainable approach has proliferated in many market sectors (particularly food) at all income levels. Some of the changes made by retailers are unseen by the consumer. Much more transit packaging is now reusable and corrugated-card outers are often replaced by multitrip plastic containers, particularly when products are distributed within large store chains. More attention is now paid to recycling used outers. To some extent this has been driven by government legislation to reduce waste as much as by any desire to adopt greener practices, but the environmental groundswell is growing. In the United States, Walmart has led the way among the large supermarket chains with a raft of environmental commitments, which include improving its truck fleet's fuel efficiency, reducing greenhouse gases, cutting energy use at its stores and reducing waste to unprecedented levels. Walmart also puts pressure on its suppliers to adopt a range of environmental and ethical standards.

WALMART

A few years ago Walmart was widely viewed as the scourge of environmentalists, and was routinely accused of squeezing suppliers and doing little to protect the rights of their workers. It now wins environmental awards and uses its influence to raise working conditions of its suppliers worldwide. Walmart has benefited from taking the environmental and ethical lead, and, as the world's largest supermarket chain, has exported its approach worldwide. Its packaging scorecard system measures several key environmental factors to assess its suppliers' environmental performance.

* *15 per cent is based on greenhouse gas/CO_2 per ton of production*
* *15 per cent is based on material value*
* *15 per cent is based on product/package ratio*
* *15 per cent is based on cube utilization*
* *10 per cent is based on transportation*
* *10 per cent is based on recycled content*
* *10 per cent is based on recovery value*
* *5 per cent is based on renewable energy*
* *5 per cent is based on innovation*

Initially the scorecard caused a certain amount of anxiety among its suppliers. This was not only because of the cost of analysis and implementation; they were also concerned that it would be a pretext for driving down their prices. Now, with compliance at over 80 per cent, it is mostly the smaller suppliers who have the most difficulty with the system, although one report indicates that compliance would cost Proctor and Gamble in the region of US$200 million.

This kind of attention by retailers to their environmental impact has led to the proliferation of life cycle analysis (LCA) specialists (see Life Cycle Analysis, p. 234), who are increasingly commissioned by manufacturers to track the total emissions and energy use of a product throughout its life and disposal.

Retailers are also helped by ongoing enhancements in the recycling infrastructure, which allow more types of packaging to be recycled. Manufacturers and retailers criticize some governments (such as those of the United Kingdom and Australia) for having a piecemeal approach to recycling – leaving it to local councils and authorities to adopt their own recycling programmes rather than implementing a national strategy. This can make it difficult for manufacturers to decide which materials to use; in effect, they are forced to make environmental decisions knowing that in some areas their packs will not be recyclable. As well as leading to labelling that is difficult to understand, this often confuses consumers. Any improvement in recycling facilities, such as the widespread recovery of drinks cartons or polypropylene, are a welcome windfall to retailers, who can improve their recycling statistics without having to make changes to their packaging formats. It would be unusual to find a supermarket or retail chain without some sort of environmental policy. Many large supermarkets offer recycling facilities and all are keen to demonstrate their green credentials.

There are many individual examples of retailers and manufacturers changing their packaging as a result of newspaper campaigns or complaints by the public, but the best incentive to use less packaging is that this will reduce their costs. With massive fuel bills it makes economic sense for packaging to be as lightweight and minimal as possible. Conflicts tend to arise over consumer perception of what environmentally friendly packaging is. Often this is down to whether it can be recycled, rather than how much energy it saves, so less environmentally friendly choices are sometimes made in deference to consumer perception (see chapter 2).

Left to their own devices and unconstrained by the law, retailers would be unlikely to have effective environmental strategies, but while they perceive that a commercial advantage will be gained by taking an environmental approach they will continue to do so. In the United Kingdom pressure from government has led to the voluntary Courtauld Commitment between WRAP (Waste Resources Action Programme) and retailers, which has galvanized industry into reducing waste. This is small beer compared to the green dot legislation originally imposed by the German government, which compelled manufacturers to make a contribution to waste disposal and ultimately created one of the world's most comprehensive and efficient recycling systems.

CONSUMERS

Consumers fall into two main categories: those who do not like packaging but will not let it change their buying habits, and those whose purchasing choices can be affected by product packaging. We will call them average consumers and environmentally active consumers.

Average consumers

While most average consumers would say that packaging is wasteful and that eco-friendly, especially recyclable, packaging is extremely important, if pressed they would probably acknowledge that packaging has some benefits. They tend to be fixated on recyclability rather than overconsumption per se, so would be unlikely to make drastic or considered changes to their purchasing decisions in order to have a more environmentally friendly lifestyle; they might make occasional green purchases if these do not involve a great deal of cost or inconvenience. Concentrated detergents, for instance, provide an environmental feel-good factor with no need for the consumer to make any real commitment. Not only do they use less liquid and often work at lower temperatures (saving energy), they involve less packaging and are easier to carry home. In the United Kingdom it has also been

Packaging is produced from a huge variety of materials, some of which is recyclable and some not

surprising how quickly and enthusiastically consumers and retailers have adapted to voluntary restrictions on using carrier bags. Being asked to pay for them has resulted in a clear shift in consumer behaviour.

For many consumers the appeal of recyclable packaging, as rubbish collections are increasingly limited by various factors like weight, the number of bags permitted per household and the frequency of collections, is that recycling reduces the burden of waste, while creating a warm feeling of having made a contribution to the environment. This motivational approach not only reduces landfill, but also increases the public's perception that it has a stake in 'saving the planet'. On the other hand, it tends to harden consumer attitudes towards non-recyclable packaging, as every item that goes into the refuse rather than the recycling bin is a visible reminder of our wasteful society or an example of overpackaging. Consumers are often annoyed when packaging is not recyclable, and frustrated when something that is routinely recycled in one part of a country has to go into the refuse bin in the area where they live. Retailers and manufacturers, usually with government sustainability targets as well as public opinion to consider, have reacted by improving the recyclability of their packaging. Some, such as Tetra Pak and Coca-Cola have invested heavily in reprocessing plants.

Though consumers are familiar with recycling, and even reusability in several Scandinavian and northern European countries, they are less conscious of other ways of benefiting the environment, such as lightweighting materials. This means that although manufacturers may fulfil government targets for materials reduction through lightweighting, as well as by reducing their energy use and transport costs, this is unlikely to make much impression on the average consumer, who cares about overpackaging without necessarily always being able to recognize it. Bottled water? No problem!

The large number of pressure groups whose aim is to reduce packaging bear testament to this primary consumer concern, and packaging excess has become a recurrent theme and cause célèbre in the media with high-profile targeted campaigns aimed at issues such as reducing the use of carrier bags. It is surprising how rapidly the media focus has shifted from food safety and dietary information to the environment. To some extent manufacturers have reacted even more quickly, partly through government pressure, but also in an effort to protect their brands from a potentially environmentally energized public. Supermarket shelves are beginning to fill with packs that are (or look) more eco-friendly.

Environmentally active consumers

Although environmentally active consumers have a negative view of packaging, they are more likely than average consumers to see it in the context of other environmental factors, such as energy use, industry emissions and deforestation, as well as food wastage.

They may use home-grown or seasonal produce rather than food that has travelled long distances, and perhaps favour local stores and markets. The source and quality of what they eat is important to them and they may well seek out Fairtrade goods. They would not support using convenience products such as bottled water or disposable nappies. They are concerned at the damage packaging does to the environment and are prepared to shun products that are overpackaged. They happily forgo a certain amount of convenience and may select less effective or more costly products with better environmental profiles. They are well informed and passionate about issues such as greenhouse gas emissions, landfill overuse, the effect of packaging on wildlife and the marine environment, as well as health issues related to packaging, such as the effects of PVC.

Despite their firmly held convictions, environmentally active consumers still consume and their choices influence manufacturers. Green detergent brands like Ecover have found themselves competing with the likes of Method and others in an increasingly large niche, and manufacturers are turning to designers to make their green products appeal to a more mainstream market.

LEGISLATORS

Legislators have a duty to protect the public, so historically their main concerns have been to inform and protect the consumer. They ensure that packaging is fit for purpose and carries the correct balance of statutory information, such as ingredients, country of origin and use-by dates. Anti-tamper legislation is widespread, offering further protection to the consumer. In the global village, where products travel freely over borders, it is often the countries with the most stringent rules that dictate the standard. A good example of how legislators have made a contribution to the environment through their work on product standards is the recent international standard for food-grade recycled plastics, opening the way for systems where packaging is delivered, collected and refilled to proliferate.

Beyond protecting the public legislators must reflect consumers' wishes and act in their interest, so a wide variety of environmental laws and directives have been passed. These, of course, vary from country to country but may include measures on issues such as overpackaging. The European Union (EU) has the most consistent environmental laws, which has led to dramatic improvements in packaging recovery throughout Europe.

Different branches of government often have differing preoccupations. For instance, in Europe at an international level the emphasis is almost entirely on reducing greenhouse gas emissions, but at a regional and national level the focus is on reducing packaging weight because of the cost of landfill – taxes on which have been driven by greenhouse gas initiatives. This, combined with legislation such as the EU's producer responsibility obligations, whereby the producer pays for the recovery or disposal of packaging, has led manufacturers to focus on reducing weight.

Extended producer responsibility (EPR), sometimes called product stewardship, is gaining ground globally, with national compliance schemes in New Zealand and Japan as well as Europe. Canada, Israel and several South American countries are looking at similar programmes. Even Korea and China, for so long apparently oblivious to environmental concerns, have enacted overpackaging laws and improved their recycling record. While many other countries lag behind, it would seem that the elephant in the room is the United States, which stubbornly resists having a national policy on packaging waste. It prefers to devolve the issue to state level; several states, such as California and Oregon, have strong environmental policies, and a number run bottle deposit schemes to improve recycling. Taking nationwide action is not necessarily a straightforward task in the United States, given the population's traditional resistance to regulation and taxation. Countries with far less environmental packaging legislation include, notably, Russia, the Gulf States and much of the Pacific Rim.

Governments are usually reluctant to do anything that could potentially harm trade, but it could be argued that more stringent packaging regulation would not only reduce the amount of packaging being produced, but would also reduce manufacturers' costs, allowing them to find other, more creative, ways to compete than by overpackaging their goods.

National recycling strategies, such as the green dot system in northern Europe, make it much easier for designers to create environmentally friendly packaging, as they can be sure the materials they use will be widely recyclable. The variable facilities for recycling seen in many countries mean the same pack could just as easily be landfilled as recycled.

This chapter has been an introduction to some of the complex issues surrounding environmentally friendly packaging. We explore some of these in more detail in the next chapters to show how they relate to packaging design. Complex issues require thoughtful solutions, which do not necessarily pander to consumer perception or packaging industry hype. We hope to point out and explore the pitfalls so that creative packaging can transcend the maze of confusion and restriction that currently surrounds it.

In the future, the material and shape of standard household objects, such as this squeeze bottle, are likely to be subjected to increased packaging regulation

CHAPTER 2

THE SEARCH FOR
ENVIRONMENTAL SOLUTIONS

THERE SHOULD NOT BE A CONFLICT BETWEEN ENCOURAGING PEOPLE TO MAKE CHOICES THAT ARE MORE ENVIRONMENTALLY FRIENDLY AND DESIGNING FOR THE RETAIL ENVIRONMENT. THE CHALLENGE IS KNOWING HOW BEST TO MAKE USE OF MATERIALS AND UNDERSTANDING THE IMPACT THEIR DISPOSAL CAN HAVE ON THE ENVIRONMENT.

REDUCE, REUSE, RECYCLE SUCCINCTLY ENCAPSULATES THE BEST WAY TO BOTH DESIGN FOR THE ENVIRONMENT AND CARE FOR IT AS A CONSUMER. IT IS AN ABBREVIATED VERSION OF THE WASTE HIERARCHY, WHICH IS WIDELY ACKNOWLEDGED TO DESCRIBE THE FULL RANGE OF OPTIONS FOR WASTE: REDUCE, REUSE, RECYCLE, RECOVER ENERGY, LANDFILL.

Reduce Create as little waste as possible to start with.
Reuse Prevent new waste being created.
Recycle Allow materials to be reprocessed and reused. This almost always consumes less energy than using virgin materials.
Recover Energy Energy recovery/incineration and composting allow the stored energy to be extracted and reused. Advances in clean-burn technology have made energy recovery more environmentally acceptable, but concerns remain over emissions.
Landfill The least attractive option, this effectively locks the waste underground, where it can still create greenhouse gases and leach toxins into the water table. Currently effort is being put into capturing the gaseous emissions and using them as an energy source.

THE WASTE HIERARCHY

Reduce

Reuse

Recycle

Recover Energy

Landfill

REDUCE

EASILY THE BEST DESIGN APPROACH IS TO USE MATERIALS WISELY AND FRUGALLY, TO AVOID HAVING TO EXPEND ENERGY AND RESOURCES ON UNNECESSARY PACKAGING. EVEN RECYCLING USES ENERGY AND RELEASES CARBON DIOXIDE, AND RELIANCE ON LANDFILL IS NOT ONLY UNWORKABLE IN THE LONG TERM BUT ALSO CREATES ITS OWN ENVIRONMENTAL ISSUES THROUGH LEAKAGE AND METHANE EMISSIONS.

Lightweighted ale bottle

The most effective ways of reducing packaging are:

• Reducing the wall thickness of materials, where possible, to save weight – known as lightweighting. This does not apply only to materials like glass, metals and plastics. Considerable advances have been made in developing lighter-weight board for card packaging. This helps not only by reducing the amount of materials used, but also saves energy during processing and transportation, not to mention costs, often with the additional benefit that the packaging can be recycled. Crucially, though, there are forms of packaging, multilayer films in particular, which are so lightweight and complex that they are not necessarily efficient to recycle. However, their minimal use of materials gives them an extremely good environmental profile.

• Considering whether products could be packed differently – moving from cans to pouches, for instance – or whether a foil-wrapped cardboard tube, however iconic, is a good way to pack potato crisps.

• Reducing the overall size of packaging to avoid wasting energy by shipping air from place to place.

• Avoiding unnecessary parts and materials. Are they needed? Less is more. In today's environmental and economic climate, packs featuring clever widgets or special functions seem somehow inappropriate.

Many consumers dislike over-fussy packaged goods, they favour simpler packs, and this is reflected in a shift to thrift. Some people realize that they can make do with less, and consuming less goes hand in hand with wasting less.

A number of types of product, such as toys, chocolates and fragrances, are consistently overpackaged, but the occasional revolt by the buying public does bring manufacturers to heel. Easter eggs, as mentioned in the introduction, were the source of controversy in the United Kingdom; they grew larger year on year, and were swathed in increasing quantities of card and plastic, reaching extremes of excess both in size and material use from the turn of the millennium. In 2009, in response to public and media pressure, manufacturers and retailers made large reductions in materials. In truth, the new Easter egg packaging did not look dissimilar from that of the 1970s – smaller sizes, more card, less plastic. But the manufacturers had the benefit of reducing their costs, and also generated a great deal of positive publicity for themselves

Realistically, though, consumers are unlikely to decide not to buy items such as electrical goods or DIY equipment simply because they do not like the packaging, so designers should make responsible packaging choices on their behalf.

IS IT REALLY NECESSARY TO SHRINK-WRAP A CUCUMBER?

One of the commonest examples of perceived overpackaging, which crops up time and again, is the humble cucumber. In the United Kingdom the Daily Mail *pursued a high-profile campaign to cajole supermarkets to remove shrink-wrapping from cucumbers, striking a blow for common sense and people power. The Women's Institute and government representatives (who know an easy target when they see one) also weighed in.*

So, how necessary is the shrink-wrapping? In short, a wrapped cucumber lasts more than three times as long as an unwrapped one: harvested, washed, transported and delivered it will stay fresh until the plastic is cut, and lose only 1.5 per cent of its weight through evaporation after 14 days, whereas an exposed cucumber loses 3.5 per cent of its weight after only three days. Shrink-wrapping means the energy-consuming process from harvesting to delivery does not have to be repeated so often, and less product ends up in landfill where it will emit damaging methane.

In adding to landfill the cucumber shares, in the United Kingdom, the fate of one-third of the food purchased, which is thrown away without being used; according to Recycle-More, the weight of food that is landfilled exceeds that of packaging waste. This is only just being widely seen as an environmental issue. Through its Landfill Directive the European Union is placing greater emphasis on the diversion of biological waste from landfill.

The issue of food wastage is by no means restricted to the European Union. A University of Arizona study in 2004 estimated that 40–50 per cent of all the food harvested in the United States is wasted; and (according to Effective-Packaging) in developing countries inadequate packaging causes 30–50 per cent of foodstuffs to decay before they reach consumers.

The Daily Mail's *nationwide campaign ultimately persuaded a major supermarket chain, the Co-op, to comply by designing transit packaging for cucumbers that does the same job as the shrink-wrap. The solution is a large, plastic, breathable liner in a cardboard box, which is claimed to keep cucumbers fresh for up to 40 days. In practice, these cucumbers do not last as long as shrink-wrapped ones, because as soon as they are put on-shelf their rate of deterioration accelerates and they continue to deteriorate in the purchaser's fridge. As for the plastic, the Co-op claim a saving of 8 tonnes a year, but they use an additional cardboard box where other retailers have reusable crates, so perhaps even the material savings are open to question.*

Can designers learn anything from this?
The cucumber and food waste controversy has sparked discussion about ways to store cucumbers and food in general, which can provide clues for designers. Some people recommend slicing the cucumber, immersing the slices in water and keeping them in the refrigerator, but one solution stands out as being particularly interesting. This is to keep the cucumber upright in the refrigerator door with the stalk end immersed in water. Unlike many other fruits, a cucumber draws water through its stem to replace the water it rapidly loses through its skin, so the solution to the perceived overpackaging of cucumbers may be as simple as selling them like flowers, from a bucket, instead of sleeving them.

The cucumber example is significant because it demonstrates that how consumers perceive materials is important in environmental retailing. Some materials, such as glass, hardly seem to register on their environmental radar, while others, particularly plastics, are never off it.

REUSE

REUSE IS OFTEN PROMOTED AS AN IMPORTANT WAY FOR CONSUMERS TO CUT DOWN ON UNNECESSARY WASTE. CERTAINLY, IT IS CONVENIENT TO BUY A FRUIT DRINK AND DISCARD OR RECYCLE THE PET BOTTLE WHEN IT IS EMPTY, BUT IF THE BOTTLE IS KEPT AND REFILLED FROM CONCENTRATE UNTIL IT IS WORN OUT, SAY FOR A MONTH, 20 OR SO BOTTLES DO NOT NEED TO BE MANUFACTURED. HOWEVER, THERE IS SOME DEBATE AS TO WHETHER PET BOTTLES CAN BE REUSED SAFELY, WHICH CONFUSES THE DISCUSSION.

Unbranded ice-cream tub

Plastic tubs for soup are not always suitable for recycling, but they can be reused in the freezer, and every time a tub is used instead of a new pack, a contribution is made to reducing packaging waste. Even in countries or areas where soup tubs can be recycled, this type of reuse would be more beneficial to the environment.

For reuse to work, however, it must make the purchase of another pack unnecessary. Simply making a bird feeder out of plastic bottles is not a useful contribution to the environment; it does nothing practical to save on packaging and the bottles will eventually end in the waste stream.

These examples are informal ways in which consumers can reuse packaging. There are opportunities for more formal reusable systems in packaging design, including various refill and closed-loop reuse systems.

REFILL PACKS

Historically, reusability has been a useful tool for selling expensive packaging. Trigger-spray packs were often initially marketed with refills so that the expensive pump could be reused. In practice, a certain number of packs had to be sold with the pump to attract new customers, and competition among manufacturers then put the convenience of the pack with the pump above thrift, consigning refills to a very small section of the market. Recently, however, the mindsets of both manufacturers and consumers have changed, so there are currently more opportunities for reusability. However, much of the success of refills will depend on customer take-up. If people are simply not prepared to buy them they will inevitably be dropped from sale, like the Body Shop's in-store refill scheme, which was taken up by only 1 per cent of its customers. There are a number of ways in which refills could be marketed.

• With a little encouragement (or competition) supermarkets could have refill bars, where customers could bring used containers to be refilled and relabelled.

Better still, supermarkets could encourage customers to return their empty bottles (some already offer loyalty points for recycling) and supply these for filling. This means a container could be used several times until it wears out.

• Powdered goods that come in glass jars or cardboard tubs could have a bag refill option; to some extent this is already happening, with instant-coffee refills.

• Several brands of detergent offer trigger-spray packs containing concentrated liquid refills that customers can dilute with tap water. This drastically reduces pack weight while encouraging customer loyalty.

In practical terms, reusable transit packaging is making the greatest contribution in this field, especially if it can be reused within the same organization. This is partly due to widespread government legislation, particularly in Europe, aimed at forcing retailers and manufactures to demonstrably reduce waste, but improved logistics have genuinely reduced costs.

REUSABLE CLOSED-LOOP AND BOTTLE-DEPOSIT SYSTEMS

Reusable closed-loop systems, such as doorstep milk deliveries in glass bottles where delivery, collection and refilling are handled by one company, usually at local level, work well on a small, local scale. The bottles can be reused up to 20 times, which means that despite being heavy in comparison to plastic, they more than make up for their additional weight in energy savings.

Another form of closed loop is the bottle-deposit scheme. In many countries such schemes for soft drinks had all but disappeared. They were expensive to run and logistically challenging, and many deposit-dependent brands died out, superseded by cheap, single-use PET bottles. However, there is now a swing away from single-use bottles to the extent that a number of countries have passed bottle-deposit laws (Bottle Bills in the United States) to encourage recycling and reuse. These are particularly prevalent in northern Europe, and often facilitate the reuse of PET bottles as well as glass ones. Germany introduced its high-profile Pfand (deposit) scheme in 2002 (with much opposition from beverage manufacturers), charging a redeemable deposit for beer and soft drinks bottles in both PET and glass, as well as aluminium cans. Refillable bottles (Mehrwegflaschen) make up a large proportion of the beverage market – both PET and glass bottles are reusable up to 25 times. Some bottle-deposit schemes even use a generic bottle style that can be relabelled and reused by several brands. Sweden, for example, uses 33-cl bottles of uniform shape. Other countries, such as the United States, Canada and Australia, have deposit systems at state level, but no national strategy. Israel is a rare exception; it has had a national scheme since 2001.

These schemes have been a conspicuous success: they have simultaneously achieved unprecedented recycling rates while reducing litter. They are of particular value in that they tend to concentrate on some of the materials most easily recycled at a regional level (glass, paper, PET bottles) and, because they are so efficient, actively encourage the growth of reprocessing.

RECYCLE

THE BENEFITS OF RECYCLING –
REDUCING ENERGY USE
AND CARBON OUTPUT, AND
FREEING-UP SPACE IN
INCREASINGLY PRESSURIZED
LANDFILL – ARE EASILY
UNDERSTOOD AND MOST PEOPLE
ARE HAPPY TO CONTRIBUTE, EVEN
IF ONLY BECAUSE HOUSEHOLD
WASTE IS INCREASINGLY
MEASURED. IT IS NOT UNUSUAL
FOR THE AMOUNT THAT IS
DISCARDED TO BE LIMITED BY THE
NUMBER OF RUBBISH BAGS
ALLOWED PER HOUSEHOLD, OR BY
WEIGHT LIMITS OR BY CONTROLS
ON DIFFERENT CATEGORIES OF
WASTE.

In many relatively prosperous regions, such as Russia and parts of the Middle East, the domestic recycling industry is still in its infancy. However, not only are improvements being made to the processes, consumers are becoming more environmentally engaged and increasingly force the pace of change. Governments worldwide are under pressure to reduce carbon emissions, so legislation is also helping to encourage use of recyclable materials and improve collection facilities.

Northern European and Scandinavian countries currently lead the way in recycling. Perhaps the most high profile and effective national recycling scheme is Germany's green dot or DSD (Duales System Deutschland). Manufacturers who sell products in Germany are compelled to pay for the retrieval of their packaging. This was initially introduced as a practical alternative to allowing consumers to return packaging to the retailer. The green dot signifies that the cost of retrieval has been paid and that the packaging can be placed in a recycling bin for reprocessing.

The Duales System Deutschland has its detractors. Although it is a non-profit organization, the cost of licensing products often rises. It is also an effective monopoly, handling the lion's share of reprocessing. Some competitors argue that it reprocesses to an uneconomical level then raises the licensing fees to cover the cost, making true competition impossible. In 2007 the European Commission ruled that the DSD should permit more competition within the recycling industry, allowing manufacturers to make separate arrangements for retrieving their packaging outside the green dot system. However, the green dot system has been adopted in most European countries in response to European Union packaging recovery requirements.

Germany has long had a special relationship with recycling, and even has special days for putting out household junk. In reality, most of the junk never makes it to the municipal recycling centre. It usually disappears before the collection truck arrives, often to reappear in

Above left:
German colour-coded recycling bins

Above:
Aluminium containers for recycling pressed into bales before processing

Opposite:
Innocent's rPET (recycled PET) bottle is 100 per cent recyclable

local flea markets. Germans habitually sort their rubbish into bins for paper, other recyclables (plastics, aluminium, tinplate, drinks cartons) and biowaste. The remainder is sent for incineration. Most glass is covered by the Pfand deposit scheme and is returnable at local retailers. Non-Pfand glass is placed in local bottle banks.

It is no surprise that Germany recycles approximately 64 per cent of its waste. However, it is not alone in northern Europe; the Netherlands, Belgium and Austria have similar figures.

Japan is similarly enthusiastic about recycling. With limited land available for landfill, incineration accounts for approximately 78 per cent of municipal solid waste, but recycling is quickly gaining ground. It is not uncommon for waste to be sorted into as many as ten categories for recycling. The town of Kamikatsu even collects 44 categories and aims to eliminate all waste going for incineration by 2020.

RECYCLING'S LIMITATIONS

In general, it is more energy-efficient to recycle and reprocess materials than manufacture them from scratch, but recycling can be an extremely variable process, which may not always be straightforward or as beneficial to the environment as might be assumed. Many materials can be recycled, but in practical terms they are limited by several considerations. Efficiency of collection, ease of sorting, efficiency of reprocessing and ultimately finding a market for the reprocessed materials determine whether recycling is possible.

Inevitably economics and legislation are factors, because governments are unlikely to bankroll inefficient recycling. If the recycled product is significantly more costly than newly processed material it simply becomes uneconomical. Both efficiency and economics can change as improved collection and reprocessing systems are developed, so what may be impractical today may be commonplace tomorrow.

Where materials are collected efficiently recycling can become the victim of its own success. Although usually government-sponsored or required by law, it is ultimately driven by commercial factors, so if supply outstrips demand the price falls to levels that threaten its commercial viability. This is currently true of steel (easily extracted from household waste by electromagnets) and paper, but can affect most materials as collection rates improve.

Efficiency of collection and ease of sorting

The popularity and use of recycling depend to a great extent on user friendliness, so for households co-mingled kerbside collections are often preferable to local recycling centres. Some environmentalists and end-users of the recycled waste argue that co-mingled recycling results in an inferior product because of cross-contamination, but this has to be balanced against its convenience for the consumer. In the United Kingdom it is not uncommon for local authorities that switch from sorted waste to co-mingled waste collections to experience a 20 per cent increase in recycling volume. However, they prefer presorted household waste because the materials can be easily sold on to reprocessors without further sorting, attracting a higher price.

Efficiency of reprocessing

Some materials are more easily reprocessed than others. Aluminium, for example, benefits from extraordinarily efficient reprocessing. Glass and steel are also easily reprocessed, and are much more efficient to reuse than virgin materials. Even clear PET is increasingly being recycled to good effect, and its manufacturers have no difficulty selling all the recycled PET (rPET) they produce to retailers and manufacturers.

Reprocessing, however, is only part of the recycling story. Each item has to be transported, sorted and cleaned, then transported again to be remanufactured. It is generally accepted that all recycled materials have a better carbon footprint than virgin raw materials, but this largely depends on how far and by what mode of transport the collected materials travel before they are reprocessed – essentially, how much fossil fuel is used in the process. For example, aluminium, glass and steel are efficiently reprocessed at a local or regional level, with considerable energy savings over packs made from virgin materials, but a great deal of plastic and paper collected for recycling ends up being shipped to the Far East from as far away as Europe and America. WRAP (Waste Resources Action Programme) reports that 80 per cent of the United Kingdom's plastic recycling and 50 per cent of its paper are sent to China.

THE CHINA SYNDROME

Much of the world's recycled waste is sent to China to be reprocessed. As an aggressively developing manufacturing economy the country needs materials. Using recycled materials is an effective way of addressing any shortfall in raw ones and the cost of manufacturing materials, so it buys huge quantities of recycled waste from around the world to reprocess it.

From the West's point of view, at first glance this seems inefficient. But the West's trade imbalance with China is such that container ships delivering Chinese-manufactured goods might make the return journey all but empty were it not for China's hunger for plastics and paper. WRAP argues that the carbon dioxide generated in the transportation of the materials from the United Kingdom is negligible, because the ships would have had to return to China with or without the plastics and paper due for recycling. It also claims that there is a net saving of carbon dioxide even if the transportation is included. However, the growing consumer perception in some countries that sending recycled waste halfway round the world to be reprocessed makes a nonsense of recycling, is damaging to the trade's credibility and makes some people reluctant to recycle.

Beyond the arguable environmental contribution of sending recycled waste to China there is the social cost. In a report on the Chinese reprocessing industry in 2001, Basel Action Network's Steve Puckett reported that conditions for workers sorting waste were poor. Children were employed to sort through bags, there was little protective clothing, and because the workers could not translate the label information they were unable to identify any toxic residue. He also reported that packaging with unidentifiable contents is often simply dumped in the countryside or burned, and that despite laws intended to prevent this there is little official enforcement and widespread corruption.

In 2005 the Daily Telegraph *reported that pieceworkers in the industrial town of Dongyang had piles of bottles dumped in front of their houses to be sorted for a wage equivalent to US$3 a day. The junkyard conditions in the town caused widespread public unrest about the pollution, which was blamed for causing high rates of cancer, miscarriages and birth defects. It is still not uncommon to see bottles piled up on the roadside ready for sorting. Many people would argue that the West was simply dumping its waste on China by proxy.*

However, this reciprocal system with the West had been working, effectively, for several years, growing incrementally year on year. China exported goods, filled its empty boats with recycled waste, reprocessed it and made more goods, or exported the reprocessed materials. Meanwhile waste, which would otherwise end up as landfill in the West, was diverted for recycling and the operators
of recycling schemes were paid well for their goods by Chinese importers.

In the autumn of 2008 the worldwide economic downturn changed the dynamic of the seemingly relentless growth of the Chinese economy. China was selling fewer goods, so did not want the recycled waste. As its price plummeted many importers who had gambled on continuous growth went bankrupt, leaving the waste piled up in China's ports. The effects were soon felt in the West as plastic and paper accumulated in warehouses. Not only was China buying less waste and paying much lower prices, it also became more selective about its quality.

As China becomes more aware of the self-harm it is inflicting and develops its home-grown recycling systems, Europe is using selective recycling to improve the quality of its locally recycled plastics. Closed-loop plants that specialize in producing recycled PET and HDPE (rPET and rHDPE) are starting to proliferate at national and regional levels. This type of plant depends on a reliably consistent supply of clear or only slightly tinted bottles, so is ideally sited near large cities or conurbations. New standards for food-grade recycled packaging have recently been agreed, so more clear bottles will be reprocessed into recyclable bottles, rather than being sent on a boat trip to China to end up as garden furniture or fleeces.

Naya water bottle of 100 per cent PET

Finding a market for the reprocessed materials

As manufacturers and retailers seek to enhance their environmental profiles, the use of recyclate – recycled materials – is increasing. The demand for rPET, for example, is high as retailers chase environmentally conscious consumers and struggle to meet government waste targets.

Clearly environmental

One of the success stories in environmental retailing has been the proliferation of clear PET, the plastic most commonly used for water and carbonated-drinks bottles. Developments in reprocessing have made it possible to recycle it in a closed loop, whereby the bottles can be recycled back into rPET. Clear PET is replacing bottles, which might previously have been manufactured in coloured HDPE, for products such as fabric conditioners. This not only increases the reservoir of potentially recyclable material, but decreases the amount of plastic going to less beneficial forms of recycling. It is not uncommon to see bottles with 100 per cent recycled PET content. The slight discolouration that is often seen can be a bonus for a brand, as it signifies that the bottle has a better environmental profile than one that is clear. How long will it be before a manufacturer uses tinted virgin plastics to give the impression of recycled plastic?

There is, however, a potential problem in that retailers and manufacturers using recycled packaging do not have to be specific about the origin of their materials, and as more and more of them seek to improve their environmental profiles they may be tempted to source their recyclate from further afield, compromising the size of their product's carbon footprint. Demand will in turn escalate costs, and increase the pressure to use more questionable sources of recyclate.

Gable-top cartons

PUBLIC PERCEPTION

However capricious and often misinformed the public may be, it is important, even essential, to take account of consumer perception. Tetra Pak is one example of a manufacturer that has done just this. It is a massive packaging empire, built on the principles of efficiency, practicality and value for money. Its beverage packaging is created at the filling plant, using a form, fill and seal process. The raw material arrives as huge preprinted spools of laminated paper, foil and plastic (or paper and plastic), so the minimum space is required to transport it, as opposed to glass bottles or cans, which have to be transported empty to the filling plant. The packs formed are usually cuboid in shape, so, although they have a larger surface area than a round bottle, they can contain a higher volume of liquid relative to the shelf space they occupy. This means that when the filled packs are transported, they take up less space. The packs are mainly constructed of paper, which, in Tetra Pak's case, comes from sustainable sources.

The problem is that, until recently, despite having several environmentally friendly attributes, after use the empty packs went into the wrong bin. They are not easily recycled because the multilayer composite material of which they are constructed cannot easily be separated. Tetra Pak is one of the world's wealthiest packaging companies, and was not in any hurry to lose ground to other more recyclable pack formats, so it has invested in massive infrastructure to reclaim its cartons and separate out the paper, plastic and aluminium foil elements for reprocessing.

Tetra Pak have clearly made an admirable commitment to recycling, yet there are questions about the environmental viability of the recovery process. The scarcity of recycling plants means the cartons often have to be transported long distances, and the amount of processing needed to recover the materials seems out of proportion to what is recovered. On the other hand, another benefit beyond reclaiming the materials, however inefficiently, is that the reprocessed cartons do not end up in landfill producing methane.

From Tetra Pak's point of view its investment means it now has an 'environmentally friendly' product that

competes on level terms with polyethylene, PET and glass bottles. This opens up design possibilities, as the juice carton-type solution becomes a potential new format for other products that are already in recyclable packs. Cereals, for instance, are already linked to beverage cartons by association (milk), so could easily make the transition to this type of packaging. Traditional bag-in-box cereal packaging has been static for many years, with just a few recent changes in proportion and the addition of windows, as demonstrated by the insightful Dorset Cereals packaging. Cartons also have a functional advantage over traditional cereal packs, because they do not contain the usually non-recyclable fiddly bag element.

While some conventional packaging materials leave much to be desired, many are acceptable from an ethical and environmental standpoint but do not benefit from the positive perception created by industry spin and the public's desire to make a positive contribution to the environment. Many of the negative environmental aspects of packaging materials are mitigated by their recyclability and performance. For instance, multilayer bags in general have particularly efficient performance relative to their weight, yet are usually non-recyclable. Aluminium is particularly energy-intensive to produce, yet highly efficient to recover from cans or trays.

THE ALUMINIUM POUCH

Comprised of both aluminium and multilayer materials, the aluminium pouch is an example of a packaging format that is affected by the detrimental perception that it is not recyclable.

The pouch has many environmentally friendly features: its lightweight format is preferable to other forms of packaging and the packs take up less space during transportation. However, it is not recyclable. And, unlike with juice cartons, there is no dominant manufacturer under threat of losing market share to recyclable pack formats, so unilateral action is not being taken to counter the negative perception. This is probably a good thing, because aluminium recovery from pouches would be nowhere near as efficient as recovery from aluminium cans or trays. Nevertheless, it would not be surprising if some sort of widespread recovery technology was underwritten by manufacturers before long. Bizarrely, they are benefiting from many pouch reuse schemes, which turn used juice pouches into handbags, shopping bags and pencil cases, but it is extremely doubtful whether this makes any meaningful environmental contribution.

From a retailing perspective, using recycled materials certainly benefits the environment. It helps achieve sustainability targets and can be used to demonstrate a commitment to greener practices. Arguably, though, in terms of customer perception it is tempting for retailers to use recyclable rather than recycled materials. For instance, some food retailers are cutting back on lightweight energy-efficient plastic trays, which may have been recycled from bottles but are usually not themselves recyclable, in favour of more widely recyclable aluminium trays.

For most consumers, being able to put packaging into the recycling rather than the waste bin is critical, so the amount of energy it takes to produce the aluminium trays compared with the plastic ones is almost irrelevant. Ultimately, given the abundance of aluminium and the depletion of plastics, combined with the negative perception of the latter, we are likely to see a great deal more aluminium packaging in the future.

Handbags made from reused aluminium pouches

THE SEARCH FOR NEW MATERIALS

POTENTIALLY, SOME OF THE MOST ENVIRONMENTALLY FRIENDLY PACKAGING IS MADE FROM BIODEGRADABLE OR COMPOSTABLE MATERIALS. THESE INCLUDE CONVENTIONAL PACKAGING MATERIALS, LIKE CARD AND PAPER, AND NEW ONES, SUCH AS BIOPLASTICS, WHICH USE PLANT MATERIALS. IT IS IMPORTANT TO STRESS 'POTENTIALLY', AS THE ENERGY USED IN THE PRODUCTION OF THESE MATERIALS, AND THEIR METHOD OF DISPOSAL, HAS A HUGE EFFECT ON THEIR ENVIRONMENTAL PROFILE.

BIODEGRADABILITY

There are several broadly similar definitions of biodegradability. According to the American Society of Testing and Materials (ASTM) a biodegradable product is 'capable of undergoing decomposition into carbon dioxide, methane, water, inorganic compounds, or biomass in which the predominant mechanism is the enzymatic action of micro-organisms that can be measured by standardized tests, in a specific period of time, reflecting available disposal conditions'.

Biomass describes a renewable energy source derived from living or recently living organisms. It can cover plant life, including food waste, forest-floor residues, paper pulp and bioplastics (derived from plants) as well as animal waste, including sewage sludge. Biomass can also be used as a source of chemicals. (**Biogas** is a gas derived from the decomposition or processing of biomass. Typically, it is mainly carbon dioxide or methane, although other trace gases can be produced.)

Fossil fuels are not considered to be biomass because their energy has been stored for millions of years and contributes to an environmental imbalance when it is released.

Not all biodegradable materials are compostable, because composting requires the creation of a beneficial,

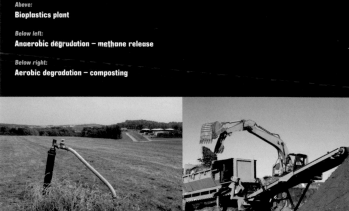

non-toxic end product within a realistic time frame and under specific operating conditions.

There are two types of biodegradation: aerobic and anaerobic.

Aerobic degradation occurs in the presence of oxygen, typically during traditional forms of composting. Microbes break biomass down into humus with water and carbon dioxide as by-products. The process is considered to be carbon neutral, because the carbon dioxide has recently been absorbed by living organisms and is effectively being re-released into the atmosphere.

Anaerobic degradation occurs in the absence of oxygen, typically in landfill sites. The material is compacted and often covered with earth. The biodegradation process is considerably slower than aerobic degradation, and the biomass emits methane and other trace gases, such as hydrogen sulphide and ammonia. Methane is 23 times more potent than carbon dioxide as a greenhouse gas.

COMPOSTABILITY

Clearly, all compostable materials are biodegradable. They can be divided into those suitable for **home composting**, and materials that require **industrial composting**, usually in a local authority facility, with the addition of heat (around 50°C/122°F) and water. It is worth stressing the difference between them as pack labelling is usually misleading.

Industrial composting facilities that will accept packaging, particularly bioplastic packaging, are few and far between. European governments are making greater efforts to improve the coverage and efficiency of composting facilities, so that more packaging can be accepted and dealt with effectively. The seedling symbol often seen on European packaging means it meets the European standard EN13432 and can be industrially composted. The packaging cannot be home or conventionally composted, so using this symbol can overstate the environmental benefits of some materials.

A European symbol for home compostable materials is in the process of being developed, along with a home composting standard, and the 'OK Home Compost' created by the Belgian industrial assessment group Vinçotte is widely used.

Home composting is very much a niche disposal method, as it depends on the consumer having the space and dedication to maintain a composter. Happily, most home compostable packaging is also recyclable. However, like other packaging marked as compostable, it may not be accepted for industrial composting as collections often focus exclusively on plant or food waste, which is easier to deal with as it breaks down more easily than other types.

Timescale

Commercial aerobic composting works on a timescale of eight to ten weeks, but coatings on card and paper can have a significant effect on how long it takes the material to break down. Unwanted items, such as sticky labels, foil, staples and plastics, all need to be effectively removed for a good-quality compost to be produced.

WRAP trials on composting suggest that cardboard at a proportion of 16 per cent to green waste degrades effectively within a normal composting time frame. A 20 per cent proportion was less successful and larger pieces of card did not fully degrade. The proportion of mixed to green waste will be an important consideration as composting develops as an alternative to landfill.

Industrial composting methods

There are several methods of industrial composting, ranging from basic to relatively sophisticated. The most common are:

Windrow composting

Long rows (windrows) of biowaste are laid out over a large open area, allowing natural ventilation. The rows are

turned mechanically to allow the material to break down, which makes the process energy-intensive but relatively inexpensive. This type of composting allows odours to escape freely, so is not suited to densely populated areas.

Aerated static pile composting (ASP)

The waste material is left open to the elements, and ventilated at the base of the pile by pipes and blowers. The process does not involve any turning, but is weather sensitive and allows odours to escape. When covered, aerated static pile composting emits fewer odours and is less sensitive to changing weather conditions.

In-vessel composting

The compost is created in an enclosed chamber or rotating drum with fan-assisted venting pipes. This is more controllable than windrow and ASP composting, as the atmosphere inside the chamber or drum can be closely monitored, and moisture and heat build-up can be controlled for optimum efficiency. Filters control emissions of odours and particulates.

Anaerobic digestion (AD)

This makes use of micro-organisms breaking down biodegradable material in the absence of oxygen. The material separates as it ferments into digestate, which is used as liquid fertilizer, and biogas with a high methane and carbon dioxide content, which can be used as a renewable energy source: it is sometimes used to heat the anaerobic digester.

Anaerobic digestion takes place in large enclosed tanks, where sewage sludge and food waste are typically processed, but is also used on farms, on a much smaller scale, for processing animal waste. Previously seen as expensive, anaerobic digestion is becoming the composting method of choice for a range of uses. It is particularly suited to disposing of food waste, which has only recently been recognized as an environmental issue because of the large quantities being sent to landfill, where it emits damaging methane. The European Union in particular is encouraging the expansion of anaerobic digestion facilities for treating food waste and biodegradable packaging, including bioplastics, which is usually unsuited to aerobic forms of composting.

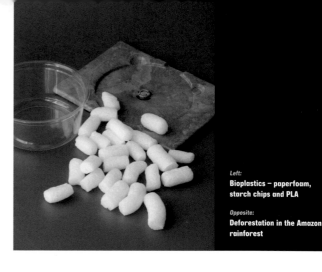

Left:
Bioplastics – paperfoam, starch chips and PLA

Opposite:
Deforestation in the Amazon rainforest

BIOPLASTICS AND BIODEGRADABLE AND DEGRADABLE PLASTICS

Biodegradable plastics are plant-based bioplastics that can be converted by micro-organisms into biomass and biogas. Not all bioplastics (see pp. 194–203), biodegrade on a timescale that makes them suitable for composting, and some plant-derived plastics, typically made from sugar cane ethanol and sometimes called green plastics, could be described as non-biodegradable, as they are effectively the same chemically as fossil plastics. Technically, they are arguably biodegradable, but the process can take hundreds of years.

Biodegradable and, to a lesser extent, degradable plastics, have some distinct advantages over conventional polymers. The floating plastic in the oceans, which breaks up slowly over many years, can be a deadly hazard to marine life, as highlighted recently by the voyage of the *Plastiki* to the North Pacific garbage patch formed in the converging currents of the North Pacific gyre. Conventional plastics break into small pieces, often releasing toxins, and are easily ingested by marine animals, but most bioplastics degrade fully within a few months. However, some environmental organizations urge caution in promoting bioplastics' biodegradability as a solution to littering, as there is the possibility this will encourage people to discard packaging in the belief that it will degrade within a few days.

Degradable plastics are conventional plastics, typically blended with starch (and other bioplastics) to accelerate their break-up or combined with chemical additives to speed up degradation. They ultimately break into pieces too small to be noticed but, critically, are not converted into biomass and biogas (see Bioplastics and recycling, p. 63).

Degradable plastics fall into three categories. They break down as the result of contact with water (hydrolytically degradable), oxygen (oxo-degradable) or light (photo-degradable). (Some bioplastics are hydrolytically biodegradable or photo-biodegradable.)

Oxo-degradable materials (usually called oxo-biodegradable by their manufacturers) are most commonly used to make plastic bags, and some experts argue that, in the oxygen-starved conditions of landfill where they will most probably end up, they will not be able to degrade

effectively. Manufacturers claim the plastic is metabolized by micro-organisms, but many scientists argue that they simply break down into pieces small enough to pass through the micro-organisms, which means the material is, strictly, degradable rather than biodegradable.

How environmentally friendly are bioplastics?

In the same way that alternative fuel production rushed headlong into biofuels, the packaging industry and public alike are being seduced by bioplastics, many of which have unresolved issues to do with their production, disposal and compatibility with current recycling systems.

Fossil fuel use All producers of bioplastics routinely claim dramatic carbon savings over fossil-based plastics, but when the energy and emissions created to produce, fertilize, harvest and irrigate the crops, and convert them to plastics, is taken into consideration the carbon savings can be minimal.

Methane The biodegradability of bioplastics is often promoted as giving them an advantage over fossil-based plastics, but if they are not composted and end up in landfill they release methane.

Land use Because new bioplastics and other biomaterials are derived from crops, they need land on which to grow. When farmland is switched to biofuel and bioplastic production it no longer produces food, which can lead to shortages and price rises, often in some of the world's poorest communities.

Deforestation Regrettably, some of the additional farmland is taken from carbon dioxide-absorbing rainforests, which further damages the planet's ability to protect itself. Bioplastics are not entirely culpable. The primary driver for increased rainforest destruction is the production of biofuels, but as bioplastics can be by-products of biofuels they cannot escape a proportion of the blame. Theoretically, the amount of land needed to grow bioplastics is relatively small compared to what is used for biofuels, but it is nonetheless significant.

Irrigation Plants need water to grow, so the diversion of sometimes scant water supplies to non-food crops like

Above: **Harvesting crops**

Right: **Fertilizing crops**

Opposite: **Drifting plastic waste**

bioplastics can have serious implications on the supply of water to food crops.

Fertilizers Intensive farming with nitrate fertilizers can contaminate waterways and release nitrous oxide, which is 300 times more damaging than carbon dioxide.

Genetic modification This is an issue for many consumers. GM crops are widely used for biofuels in particular, but not all bioplastics. However, there is little to guarantee a GM-free source. Some of the larger bioplastics producers, such as Novamont, Natureworks and Plantic are GM-free, and Europe and China produce non-GM crops. Genetically modified sugar cane and maize are common in the Americas.

Compostability Bioplastics are usually compostable, but often only in an industrial facility where they are treated with a combination of heat and water not present in a home composter.

Bioplastics and recycling

Most composting plants are currently unlikely to accept anything that looks like plastic, so, given that bioplastics are unlikely to reach an industrial composting facility, they will either end up with the general waste destined for landfill, where they will emit methane as they break down, or be mixed with and contaminate conventional plastics destined for recycling. PET bottles, in particular, which are widely sorted for recycling, are exposed to the threat of contamination by identical, clear PLA (polyactic acid) bioplastic bottles. When mixed with PLA the structural properties of the resulting recyclate are undermined, since even a small amount of degradable material can seriously weaken it.

If bioplastics are going to make a meaningful contribution to packaging there needs to be a better infrastructure of industrial composting plants and improved labelling, otherwise bioplastic packaging will continue to languish in landfill sites emitting damaging methane. In 2008 approximately only 1 per cent of bioplastics in Europe were composted, but European

lawmakers are seeking to improve composting and digestion facilities. The European Commission (EC) Landfill Directive aims to remove 65 per cent of organic waste from landfill by 2016.

In theory, bioplastics fit very neatly into a problem area in recycling. Despite being unsustainable, conventional oil-based plastics are recyclable. However, there are so many different but similar-looking plastics, as well as multilayer plastic films, that it is not practical to collect more than a few easily identifiable and economically viable ones for recycling. There are also issues with contamination by food and the efficiency with which they are recovered that prevent some conventional plastics being widely recycled. So it is not easy to recycle anything like 100 per cent of the oil-based plastics that are produced. Crucially, because these films, food-contact and multilayer plastics are unlikely to be destined for the recycling chain, which is also incompatible with bioplastics, there is a clear delineation that could be a gateway to the wider introduction of bioplastics in place of some fossil-based plastics. Their poor performance in comparison to conventional plastics is a major drawback, which will need to be resolved, but progress continues to be made.

Although the problems with bioplastics are not insurmountable, there appears to be an industry-wide realization that they are not the miracle plastics that were hoped for and hyped. This is combined with an equally widespread determination to ignore their negative aspects and (literally) plough on regardless. There is too much to be gained by appeasing the public desire for apparently 'sustainable' products.

OTHER ENVIRONMENTAL SOLUTIONS

THE SEARCH FOR ENVIRONMENTAL SOLUTIONS HAS LED TO GENUINE PROGRESS BEYOND NEW MATERIALS AND IMPROVED RECYCLING. CONCENTRATES, FOR EXAMPLE, ARE BECOMING A POPULAR WAY OF SELLING DETERGENTS. THE CONCENTRATED LIQUID IS CHEAPER TO PACK AND TRANSPORT, USES LESS ENERGY IN THE PROCESS AND OFTEN WASHES AT LOWER TEMPERATURES.

Concentrated drinks like squashes will conceivably become more popular; concentrated fruit drinks for adults are moving from niche towards mainstream. There are signs that machines to make fizzy drinks at home could return to take on the massive carbonated-drinks market, which is mainly a vehicle for selling water. Certainly Soda-Club/SodaStream make more noise about saving the planet than they do about saving money.

SodaStream and SodaStream concentrate

65

ENERGY RECOVERY AND INCINERATION

ENERGY RECOVERY AND INCINERATION ARE AT THE BOTTOM OF THE FOOD CHAIN WHEN IT COMES TO ENVIRONMENTALLY FRIENDLY SOLUTIONS TO DEAL WITH WASTE, BUT GRADUAL IMPROVEMENTS AND SOME NEW DEVELOPMENTS ARE CREATING A SHIFTING LANDSCAPE.

Incinerator at Solingen, Germany

Recovering energy from waste, sometimes called Waste to Energy (WtE), is usually based on incineration. Many European countries use this as a primary means of waste disposal. Germany, for instance, recycles or reuses most of its packaging, but what is left is more likely to be incinerated than sent to landfill. Incineration is particularly suited to smaller countries, such as Japan, where the amount of available land is limited.

Incineration, however, does not normally have a good press. Doubts over the process include fears about the release of dioxins and heavy metals, and the toxicity of the ash which may have to be disposed of in specialist sites. Municipal incinerators tend to be seen as monolithic industrial leviathans spewing noxious gases. Although these still exist there has been a quantum leap in incinerator technology. High-efficiency, 'clean' incinerators can generate energy from waste and significantly reduce the bulk of any that is going to landfill. Despite contributing to carbon dioxide and other gaseous emissions, their filtration systems and controlled environment mean that only a fraction of the gases end up in the atmosphere. A German study found that in 1990 over one-third of dioxin emissions came from incinerators, but by 2000 the figure had fallen to less than 1 per cent. Dioxin emissions from private households now dwarf those from incinerators by a factor of 20.

Incinerators therefore need not be banished to out-of-town industrial wastelands. The Austrian Spittelau WtE plant is not only located in the centre of Vienna, it is also a tourist attraction. Its exterior was designed by the Viennese artist Friedensreich Hundertwasser, who later designed the Maishima incineration plant in Osaka, Japan, which also became a tourist destination.

While it could not be argued that city incinerators are always uncontroversial – even in Vienna – they certainly demonstrate how energy recovery through incineration can be made more acceptable. The Spittelau plant created new emission standards for incinerators, with 99.9 per cent of particles removed by filtration. The hot water it

creates supplies a district heating system and the total energy generated is sufficient to meet the needs of 15,000 homes. Even the ash residue is used in building materials such as bricks. Energy recovery through incineration often goes hand in hand with materials recovery, so anything recyclable is recovered and the rest goes for incineration.

The by-products of incineration are energy and ash, both of which have benefits for the environment. Incinerating waste allows its stored energy to be released and put to good use driving turbines to generate electricity. The high levels of heat mean many types of clinical and hazardous waste can be disposed of safely. The remainder of the burned waste – the ash – needs to be sent to landfill, but its bulk is reduced by 90 to 95 per cent, making it easier to deal with, and because it has been incinerated it will not continue to emit greenhouse gases over decades.

However safe they can be made, an incinerator will never be a popular addition to the local community, but

inevitably pressure on landfill, as well as increasingly limited options for exporting waste, will make incineration an essential option for both government and local authorities. The types of packaging most likely to be processed at a WtE plant are paper and plastics or combinations of the two.

Waste paper, either poorly sorted or contaminated by food and other materials, can make up a significant proportion of landfilled municipal solid waste – approximately 35 per cent in the United Kingdom and about 40 per cent in the United States – and emits methane into the atmosphere as it degrades. Incinerating paper and using it as a fuel not only makes economic sense, but limits its harmful effects on the atmosphere.

Plastics, too, have potential energy value which is safely released in modern WtE plants, although many people would argue that they have far less potential for emissions when they are left in landfills, and are more usefully recycled using the newest technology. Bioplastics emit methane in landfills and are usually not accepted for composting, so energy recovery is currently the most effective form of disposal. Films in the form of bags, shrink-wrap labelling and lidding are usually not recycled, so they also lend themselves to energy recovery processes.

OTHER FORMS OF ENERGY RECOVERY

There are several different types of energy recovery system other than conventional incinerators, including plasma arc, pyrolysis and gasification, and anaerobic digestion.

Plasma arc

Waste between two electrodes is superheated to a temperature of 1,300°C (2,372°F) by an electrical current, which effectively vaporizes it and creates solid waste and syngas (synthetic gas), which can be used as a feedstock for the petrochemical industry or a fuel in its own right. Plasma arc is in its infancy, so there are relatively few plants operating, and there are questions over whether the process uses more energy than it creates.

Pyrolysis and gasification

Pyrolysis and gasification are new technologies for treating waste, and more efficient in their production of energy than incineration. Their main product is syngas.

Pyrolysis is a process where waste is thermally degraded in the absence of oxygen. Gasification uses extremely high temperatures and some oxygen, but the waste does not combust.

Although energy recovery using these technologies may be more efficient than incineration, reducing waste to around 8 per cent of its original bulk and relieving pressure on landfill, there is still the potential for harm to the environment because carbon dioxide and toxins are generated as exhaust gases. Friends of the Earth reports that pyrolysis and gasification create less environmental damage than conventional incinerators, but both processes depend on paper, food waste and plastics, so there is some concern that this could undermine recycling efforts.

Anaerobic digestion

Anaerobic digestion, discussed earlier as a form of composting (see p. 59), produces significant quantities of methane, which is usable as an energy source.

LANDFILL

LANDFILL IS IN GENERAL NO
LONGER A PROCESS WHEREBY
RUBBISH IS SIMPLY POURED INTO
A CONVENIENT HOLE
IN THE GROUND, SUCH AS
A WORKED-OUT QUARRY.
ALTHOUGH THERE ARE MANY
EXCEPTIONS, LANDFILL SITES ARE
USUALLY PROPERLY PLANNED AND
REGULATED. THEY ARE PREPARED
WITH A MEMBRANE OF CLAY,
INTENDED TO PREVENT LEACHATE
(RAINWATER MIXED WITH LIQUID
TOXINS AND BIOMASS) AND
LANDFILL GASES ESCAPING INTO
THE WATER TABLE. DRAINS ARE
LAID TO COLLECT THE LEACHATE
AND VENTS INSTALLED TO COLLECT
METHANE AND OTHER GASES
CAUSED BY CHEMICAL REACTIONS.

These can be flared off to prevent them escaping, or collected for reuse as an energy source. Each day, after the waste has been compacted It is covered with a blanket of soil or wood chippings to prevent emissions and allow the process of anaerobic microbial digestion to begin.

The preparation and process is much more labour-intensive than in the past, so costs can be significant. Landfills are also targets for taxation, as an incentive for local authorities and industry to operate more efficient recycling schemes or to encourage manufacturers to produce more efficient or recyclable packaging. European legislation actively discourages their use through the European Union's Landfill Directive, which is aimed at reducing the negative effects landfill has on the environment. This includes efforts to limit the amount of methane-producing biological waste, as well as toxic waste which can leak into groundwater.

In recent years landfill sites have been exploited as energy sources. For instance, a huge site north of Los Angeles extracts biogas via pipes buried deep within the waste mound and sends it directly to a power plant, where it produces enough energy to power 2,500 homes, and is sometimes used to power municipal vehicles, including garbage trucks. However, there are more efficient ways of producing biogas. It could be argued that the large amounts collected in landfills are testament to the failure to make use of existing and developing technologies and processes.

Landfill sites have been a convenient sticking-plaster solution to the growing crisis in the disposal of waste, but in the long term there are no guarantees that they will continue to be monitored and managed effectively. They can potentially remain toxic for hundreds of years. However well managed a landfill site, and however well prepared the walls and floor to prevent leakage, there is always a likelihood, even inevitability, that over time leachate and gases will contaminate the surrounding area and, most disturbingly, enter watercourses.

In many countries there simply is not enough available land to continue using landfill at the current rate and, partly out of necessity, Europe has been especially proactive in developing alternative waste strategies. But in the United States, where there is an abundance of land, the arguments against landfill are not always so straightforward. After all, if left untaxed landfill is considerably cheaper than more efficient waste strategies that require huge investment in infrastructure. It is easy to understand the temptation to keep building landfill sites, and dressing them up as green with biogas-to-energy schemes. Certainly, organized properly, landfill sites could be a valuable source of materials to be recovered in the future.

PLASTIC MINING

Although plastic packaging is often recyclable, many types of plastic are so difficult to collect efficiently and economically that they are simply dumped in landfill, where they will take hundreds of years to break down. Almost all the plastics ever produced are still around in some form or other, but, given the time it takes for them to break down, they release carbon extremely slowly, so to a certain extent have been taken out of the carbon-emission cycle. Plastics are widely used as building

materials precisely because they last so long. Oil may disappear within a few years, but plastics will be around in abundance, locked away in waste tips. Landfill sites could be the plastic mines of the future, and are reserves that will not dry up quickly.

Recovering plastics from landfills will not be entirely straightforward: methane and other gases will have to be contained or allowed to die down, for example. However, mining for plastics is already considered an option for recovering ones that are currently recycled. Recyclable plastics were sent to landfills for many years before today's recycling infrastructure was developed, so when prices paid for plastics are high, mining the sites for recyclable types becomes an attractive option. In the United Kingdom landfill sites from the 1980s are laid out so that hazardous waste areas are clearly separated, and have sufficient amounts of recoverable plastics (as well as aluminium and other non-ferrous metals) to make mining them potentially worthwhile. The need for methane emissions to dissipate means this could not begin until around 2030, but by then the price of plastics could make mining cost-effective.

It would be advisable to collect and separate all plastics in dedicated landfill sites now, so that they are easier to recover when the oil finally runs out. In time, plastics that are currently unusable may well be recoverable with new technologies. When plastics start to run out there will be the kind of rush to innovation that is now being applied to developing new energy sources, such as biodiesel from algae which avoids replacing food crops with fuel crops.

Packaging is a global problem and requires a global solution. Bioplastics may be part of the answer to the search for greener, environmentally friendly packaging, but localized reprocessing, energy recovery and material reduction will all have a role to play. Legislation and national regulation may be the key to resolving some of the conflicts that limit environmental advances. Perhaps more countries should adopt bottle-deposit schemes or have national strategies for waste recovery, rather than the

Landfill liner

piecemeal local schemes most of them currently pursue. These often make a nonsense of material choices for designers and create confusion for the consumer.

A successful strategy will be multipronged, based on continuous innovation in both manufacture and disposal combined with proper evaluation and regulation that truly improves the environmental profile of packaging, rather than the emotionally charged scatter-gun approach of today.

CHAPTER 3

DESIGNING CREATIVE ENVIRONMENTALLY FRIENDLY PACKAGING

THERE IS INCREASING PRESSURE FROM CLIENTS TO PRODUCE ENVIRONMENTALLY FRIENDLY PACKAGING SOLUTIONS. SO MUCH SO THAT IT IS RARE FOR PACKAGING DESIGNERS TO RECEIVE A PROJECT BRIEF THAT DOES NOT INCLUDE 'ENVIRONMENTALLY FRIENDLY' AS ONE OF ITS MAIN CRITERIA. CLIENTS FEEL THE PRESSURE FROM BOTH GOVERNMENT AND PUBLIC OPINION, BUT THEY ARE ALSO CONCERNED TO DO THE RIGHT THING. OF COURSE, THERE ARE THOSE WHO SEE GREENING-UP AS A MARKETING OPPORTUNITY, AND THIS IS ACCEPTABLE PROVIDED IT DOES NOT LEAD TO DISINGENUOUS SOLUTIONS THAT MISLEAD THE PUBLIC. A PACKAGING DESIGNER SHOULD FOCUS ON CREATIVE SOLUTIONS THAT ARE PROFITABLE FOR THE CLIENT, BUT AT THE SAME TIME TAKE CARE TO PURSUE THE GREENEST SOLUTIONS POSSIBLE.

IN THIS CHAPTER WE LOOK AT THE BEST WAY TO NEGOTIATE THE ENVIRONMENTAL MAZE – BALANCING PROFITABILITY AND CREATIVITY WITH SENSITIVITY TO THE ENVIRONMENT. THERE IS NO DOUBT THAT DESIGNING GREENER PACKAGING CAN BE FRUSTRATING AND POTENTIALLY LIMITING, BUT IT IS POSSIBLE TO TRANSCEND AND EXPLOIT THE LIMITATIONS TO PRODUCE INNOVATIVE, INSPIRATIONAL AND JUST PLAIN BETTER PACKAGING, WHILE CARING FOR THE ENVIRONMENT.

BRAND RECOGNITION AND OWNERSHIP

FIRST AND FOREMOST, PACKAGING MUST BE FIT FOR PURPOSE. IT HAS TO PROTECT AND PRESERVE THE PRODUCT IT CONTAINS THROUGH ALL STAGES OF TRANSPORTATION, IN THE RETAIL ENVIRONMENT AND RIGHT THROUGH TO THE TIME THE CONSUMER OPENS IT. HOPEFULLY, A PACK WILL DO MUCH MORE THAN THIS BY ADDING VALUE TO THE BRAND WITH ENGAGING GRAPHICS, A DRAMATIC PACK STRUCTURE OR IMPROVED FUNCTIONALITY.

Examples of efficient packaging

Ownership comes through creating distinctive design elements in packaging, but from a manufacturing and marketing perspective there are persuasive arguments for uniformity, and the structural design of packaging has always been subject to restrictions. Most packs involve some sort of factory process to a lesser or greater degree, and the most efficient ones for packing, shipping and retailing are based on a uniformly inflexible pack structure.

Some of the most commonly used basic pack types for food are: cans, beverage cans, milk/juice cartons, plastic bags and, more recently, doy bags (pouches, for example, for soup). Their advantages are that they make use of fast, high-volume, cheap packaging processes that allow efficient transportation and handling. Most of these more restrictive pack formats have a good environmental profile, as they are either recyclable, more efficient or use minimal materials. Many materials that can be recycled are not retrievable in quantities that are viable, and the extent to which mass-produced pack formats are used means they often lend themselves to widespread recycling.

Their disadvantage is that the only variable that allows brand and product differentiation is the graphic treatment, which is not to be underestimated but is only a part of building a brand. Uniformity is the enemy of a brand, so however different the product and impressive a pack design may be, a pack will always be seen in the context of other packs in the on-shelf shouting match.

With the marketplace saturated by basic pack types, in which manufacturers have already made a significant investment, and consumer focus firmly fixed on sustainability, it seems that manufacturers are often reluctant to experiment with pack shape, despite recent research that suggests presentation and functionality are as important to consumers as environmental performance (Perception Research Services 2008).

If a designer is to get beyond these restrictions and design creative environmentally friendly packaging, there are a number of approaches to follow, including modifying existing standard pack shapes, improving functionality, lightweighting and using recyclable and recycled materials. These will be discussed later in this chapter, together with ways in which designers can communicate their environmental credentials. Finally, we discuss the necessity of keeping up to date in this fast-moving area.

THE DESIGN PROCESS

DESIGNERS (AND SPECIFIERS) MAY HAVE DIFFERENT APPROACHES TO A PROJECT, BUT BOTH WANT TO PRODUCE WORK THEY CAN BE PROUD OF WHILE KEEPING THEIR CLIENT HAPPY. THEY ARE USED TO WORKING TO DETAILED BRIEFS, FINDING SOPHISTICATED WAYS TO INTERPRET THE CLIENT'S REQUIREMENTS AND, IF NECESSARY, ARE PREPARED TO ARGUE FOR SOLUTIONS THAT PUSH THE BRIEF IN UNEXPECTED DIRECTIONS.

The dialogue between designer, specifier and client may involve collaborative brainstorming, mood boards and consumer research but in the end, whether a design is chosen after weeks of discussion in focus groups or because the managing director likes blue, there should have been a comfortable process based on interpreting criteria, such as: Who is the product intended for? Where will it sell and for what cost? Does it hang or stack?

Although there is almost always some sort of environmental requirement in a packaging brief, more often than not specific aims are sketchy. A client may not know how much environmental input to expect from the designer. Designers can be coy about probing the background of the client's environmental requirements. These may be rooted in government legislation, industry commitments, company policy or consumer perception, but it is crucial for the designer to glean as much information as possible about the client's environmental needs so that they can be considered from the beginning of the project. Despite the wealth of good intentions from retailers and manufacturers there are varying depths of understanding, so the designer may have to discuss the environmental options with the client in some detail.

Sometimes the client's perception of their product needs to be re-evaluated. A small amount of probing can reveal fertile ground for exploration. For instance, if window film can be removed from a carton design this not only reduces the number of materials used and makes the carton easier to recycle, but the customer is able to interact more closely with the product.

There are, of course, many occasions when a product needs to be fully enclosed, typically for hygiene or security reasons, but clients can sometimes be overzealous in second guessing retailers' requirements. Many baby products, including clothes, for example, are fully enclosed, but if a baby garment is viewed as just a garment this becomes unnecessary. Once that simple observation has been made opportunities for material reduction and interaction with the product follow.

Waitrose glasses packs

Waitrose Outdoor Living plastic glasses assembly

MEETING ENVIRONMENTAL AIMS

Creativity, cost and practicality have always had a tense relationship, which designers and specifiers routinely struggle to resolve. Throwing the environment into the mix inevitably has the potential to ruffle feathers. Any project typically involves a marketing representative, an account director and a production engineer, but seldom an environmental champion. Designers need to make clear to their colleagues or clients how they have reached their environmental decisions, and be prepared to challenge dubious suggestions based largely on cost or convenience in much the same way that they would argue for other aspects of their designs.

On the other hand, the perfect is the enemy of the good. When the chips are down cost or brand presence are often the key drivers for a product so, however elegant the designer's environmental solution, the client may opt for what they consider is the least risky, status quo route, perhaps the use of slightly less material or materials that are slightly more sustainable. Any progress is progress, and in fast-moving consumer goods (FMCG) retailing small material reductions can amount to saving hundreds of tonnes a year.

Designers must be realistic about environmental aims. Not all clients want to change the world; they may want to do only the bare minimum to comply with legislation or give an enhanced impression of sustainability. But, however unenthusiastic they may be, progress can usually be made without adding cost or drastically altering manufacturing processes; and the chances are the client will not only be delighted with the result, but will also make public relations capital from the changes.

Some clients may be extremely enthusiastic about their environmental image, and perhaps have preconceived ideas about some of the high-profile eco-materials now available. They need to be guided through their key requirements, starting with functionality. For instance, if they have a food product, can it be effectively sealed? What barrier properties does the chosen material have? Can the pack be gas-flushed to extend the product life? In other words, will the product suffer? If these issues can be addressed satisfactorily the environmental merits of the material concerned can then be discussed.

However, caution is still required. Plenty of materials suppliers offer quick-fix feel-good environmental packaging solutions at the right price, but this may amount to self-deception or, worse, consumer deception. Designers and specifiers have a duty to the client to, at least, look out for and flag up any potential pitfalls.

An enthusiastic client can turn a designer into his or her own worst enemy – keen to push the boundaries, but sometimes unwary of the potential consequences – so it is important to keep asking whether a solution is green or simply cool. For example, investing in products with a dubious second life or after-use is the easiest trap to fall into. If a pack cleverly turns into something useful, but is something a customer would never otherwise buy, it is no more than single-use packaging in disguise. For after-use to work it has to encourage some sort of saving. This seems obvious, but it is easy to delude oneself (and the client).

BE SCEPTICAL ABOUT MANUFACTURERS' CLAIMS FOR THEIR PACKAGING MATERIALS AND PRODUCTS

It is always best to take manufacturers' claims for new 'miracle' materials with a pinch of salt. Do some research to see whether they have been independently assessed. Manufacturers usually leave out the best reasons not to use their material. Find out whether special equipment is needed on the packaging line to accommodate the pack format. Does the new material have printing restrictions? Does it have adequate barrier properties? Will it seal effectively? Will it lead to additional secondary packaging (outer boxes or layer supports)? Is it recyclable or sustainable? For example, if a manufacturer claims to make a biodegradable plastic from plants the questions to ask are:

Does it work as well as conventional plastics?
How much fossil fuel is used in its production?
Is the crop genetically engineered?

WINE GLASSES

W

GLASSES ARE TRAPPED AT BASE

Concept sketches for the Waitrose Outdoor Living wine-glass pack

Is the plastic recyclable?
Where was it produced?
How easily does it compost?

IN-HOUSE GUIDELINES

A growing number of companies have strict environmental packaging policies. This applies particularly to multinationals trading in regions where there are stringent government policies on waste. Other companies may simply have a more high-profile green agenda, so packaging policy is an important part of their offer.

Where companies have specific corporate guidelines covering the amount of recycled or recyclable materials to be included in the packaging, it is especially important to consider these requirements from an early stage of the design process to avoid a desperate, last-minute scramble to achieve compliance. They should be treated like other design parameters, such as cost, shelf height or volumetric capacity – not obsessively, but recognizing that they have huge potential to cause difficulties at a later stage if ignored, or to help shape the design if embraced.

Frustratingly, the targets set by such guidelines often tend to focus on recycling, whereas lightweighting or

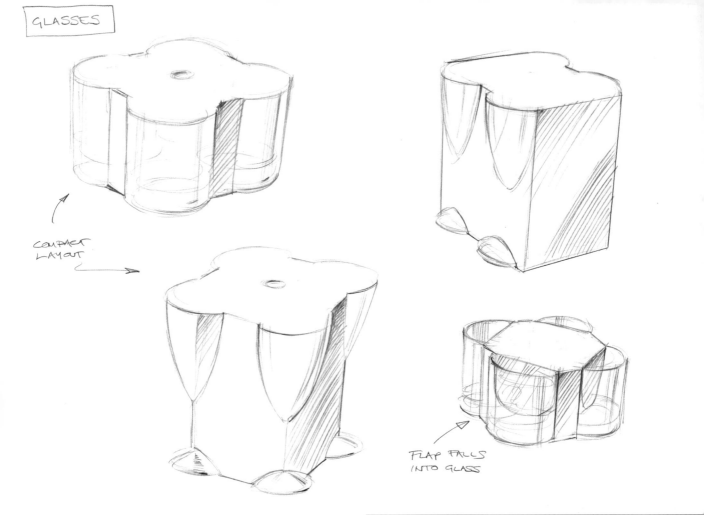

COMPACT
LAYOUT

FLAP FALLS
INTO GLASS

Concept sketches for the Waitrose Outdoor Living packs

pack-size reduction can be of more benefit. On the other hand, encouraging the market for recycled materials helps to stimulate their collection. It is the designer or specifier's job, as much as the project manager's, to recognize the environmental bottom line and make sure it remains achievable; otherwise the odds are the design will suffer in order to meet the minimum environmental requirement.

There is an assumption that eco-design is somehow different to conventional forms of design; perhaps that the creativity bar is set lower. Of course, there are many examples of the eco-design solution being simply to put the product in a grainy-looking carton or pulp tray. But poor design is poor design. Brands need personality, not homogeneity. The process of designing eco-packaging is essentially no different from designing any other form of packaging, yet in designing for the environment there needs to be a heightened level of communication between designer and client, and in some cases a little more time for development.

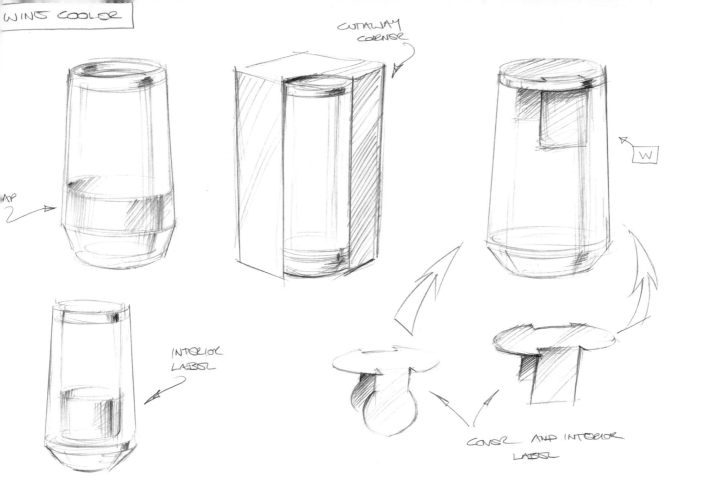

WINE COOLER

CUTAWAY CORNER

MAP

INTERIOR LABEL

W

COVER AND INTERIOR LABEL

1. INFORMATION/RESEARCH

Without proper preparation the process of designing environmentally friendly packaging can be fraught with compromise. The first step is to be clear about what is required environmentally. The client may be vague about specific needs, so all options should to be discussed.

It is particularly important to acquire as much information as possible about the potential of the packaging process so that the designer can balance a creative approach with a sound knowledge of the potential limitations.

For instance, when a supermarket chain or store commissions an own-brand product the retail buyers usually dictate the design of the packaging. Sometimes, though, large-volume suppliers that provide several big retailers with similar products have the whip hand. Often they are prepared to make only small changes to accommodate the retailer, because they are constrained by their existing production line. Even if changes are possible the supplier may be reluctant to slow down production to accommodate a new line set-up for one client. Either way, the limitations have to be worked around.

Production managers are not always proactive in suggesting solutions to design issues, so a little bit of knowledge about how a product is made can help win them over. It is always a good idea to visit the factory if possible, but if time, budget or distance prevent this it is best to get a full description of the line capabilities at an early stage of the design process.

What a manufacturing client may see as a simple request can often have far-reaching consequences for a pack design. For example, a free-standing pack that can hang or stack, required because the client needs to ensure that the product can be sold in a wide range of formats to suit different retail environments, may well be more environmentally challenging than one that only hangs.

If a client is tied to a specific geographic manufacturing location, this can affect the types of material suited to the packaging for their product. There is little point in racking up excessive energy miles transporting environmentally friendly materials to a manufacturer on the other side of the globe.

2. CONCEPTS

Sketching out ideas is probably the most critical stage of the design process and perhaps the one least appreciated by clients. It is important to find the widest possible range of solutions for a given product within a realistic framework for production. For instance, if unusual materials are being considered it is important first to establish whether they are suited to the intended purpose and are locally available to the manufacturer.

When the sketches are reviewed it is essential to ensure that the designs presented to the client are realistic. All too often, the focus is on presenting something spectacular and the details are sidestepped. Sometimes a design that looks feasible at the outset can be impossible to manufacture on an existing production line, or is so diluted in development that it becomes unrecognizable.

Any new or unfamiliar materials must be fully researched to ensure that they will function effectively and fulfil the client's environmental criteria within realistic cost parameters.

3. DEVELOPMENT

It is all too easy to become locked into a process that is bound to end in compromise, so it is important not to lose focus. It is essential to seek, and be able to adapt to, feedback. For instance, it is sensible to consider making changes in a carton design so that more cartons can be cut from a single piece of card, or to soften radii on a glass bottle to help reduce wall thickness.

The process of lightweighting materials such as glass and plastic is extremely shape sensitive, so with this type of brief it is helpful to have a good relationship with the bottle manufacturer. This will facilitate a certain amount of give and take, and make it easier to avoid ending up with an efficient but anodyne shape. Additional time needs to be allowed for trialling lightweighted designs. These types of project can be extremely frustrating without the manufacturer's co-operation.

Ideally, the designer should be able to walk the client through the whole process of designing the pack, sourcing the material and developing it through to production by liaising with the manufacturer. In any project, designers have to be champions for their creations when others find reasons to water down their designs – and never more so than when designing environmentally friendly products, which may involve unfamiliar materials and processes, higher costs and longer lead times.

4. EVIDENCE

A client is expected to care about the bottom-line cost of producing a new pack. Equally, when environmentally friendly packaging is being designed it is not unreasonable for the client to want to know how the environment is being helped. Increasingly, retailers are also demanding information about energy consumption for the products they sell.

If a new design is based on the same materials as the previous one it is easy enough to evaluate where savings have been made. However, when a totally new type of pack is being considered – rPET instead of lightweighted glass, for example – some form of more detailed analysis may be needed.

Life cycle analysis can be essential in comparing outcomes (see p. 234). Several software programs make rough comparative judgements between materials without needing to be supplied with all the external factors involved. Of course, it may be necessary to prepare a full analysis, factoring in carbon emissions for the entire supply chain, retailing and disposal. This increasingly expanding specialist field is currently a source of some controversy because of its varying forms of methodology, but as common industry standards are developed it will become an indispensable service for designers and manufacturers.

SHOULD DESIGNERS BOYCOTT CLIENTS WHO ROUTINELY OVERUSE PACKAGING?

Taking a stand on environmental principles can be tricky. It is not unusual for designers to shun commissions from alcohol or cigarette manufacturers, and, certainly, individuals within design consultancies are not necessarily required to be involved with these types of project. Given that many designers are concerned about the effect packaging can have on the environment, perhaps they should have the option to refuse work on environmental grounds. However, it would be difficult to make a convincing case that overpackaging can harm the public as directly and demonstrably as cigarettes and alcohol.

Ultimately, rejecting work for environmental reasons will always be down to the company policy of the design consultancy or the conscience of the individual designer, but there is an argument that this type of approach (or reproach) would add to the pressure on manufacturers to address the environmental profile of their packaging. On the other hand, the more opulent or overpackaged a product the more scope for improvement. Designers and specifiers are in a unique position to be guerrilla environmentalists. If they can impress a client by using greener packaging they will not only improve the product in hand, but will also have a platform to build on for other projects.

Manufacturers do not necessarily prefer overpackaging. More probably, they are locked into the defensive mindset that if they use less packaging in their particular sector they will lose market share or their product will look less attractive than those of their competitors. 'Me too' is a powerful force in retail, so designers have to work hard to overcome client prejudices by showing that more packaging is not the same as better packaging. Saving the client money is a good place to start.

We will now return to methods a designer can use to create environmentally friendly packaging.

CONSIDER THE EFFECT OF SHAPE

PACK SHAPE IS IMPORTANT FOR MANY REASONS, INCLUDING HANDLING EFFICIENCY, SAVINGS ON MATERIALS AND ITS EFFECT ON OUTER PACKAGING. IF A PACK IS STACKABLE IT CAN SAVE SECONDARY PACKAGING MATERIALS (LAYER DIVIDERS) AND MAKE IT GENERALLY EASIER TO HANDLE IN TRANSIT AND TO DISPLAY ON-SHELF. THE STRONGER THE PACK, THE HIGHER PALLETS CAN BE STACKED, LEADING TO EFFICIENCY SAVINGS.

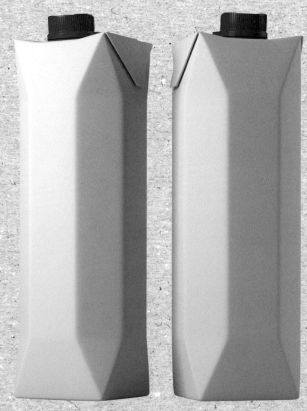

Packaging for lubricants for car engines, for example, is generally designed to withstand being stacked several pallets high, usually with only a film wrap to prevent the packs moving. Smaller packs are often arranged on corrugated trays with a lightweight film wrap. Their inherent structural strength facilitates this minimal outer packaging, saving weight and materials.

Juice and milk cartons are extremely efficient; they waste little space, which means less air is moved from place to place, and are easy to transport and display. However, they are are sculpturally anonymous, which places greater emphasis on the graphics for brand differentiation.

On the other hand, a round footprint is the most efficient shape for moulding bottles. It has the maximum strength for minimum wall thickness, and so saves on materials. Bottles for carbonated drinks are almost always cylindrical. Additional curved detailing and panelling is used to add strength and can be a useful design feature.

Although plastic bottles with a squarer footprint are less structurally robust, they are more space-efficient for transportation than round ones as there is less air between them. Milk and juice bottles are good examples. Because their contents are basic staples they are usually the only brand on offer in-store, so are not taking part in a beauty contest. Their shape and size are constrained by the internal dimensions of a standard refrigerator, which means they need to be as space-efficient as their functionality will allow.

Left:
Large PET carbonated-drink bottles

Opposite:
Shaped beverage cartons

Above:
The evolution from the classic Heinz glass bottle, to the polyethylene bottle, to the easy-squeeze tottle

Opposite:
The development of the Orangina bottle in France

Often a design requirement for bottles is that they must have either straight sides or two points of contact so that they travel down the filling line without falling over. Irregularly shaped or wide-shouldered bottles have become more prevalent in recent years. The cost and production issues that often restricted this type of design in the past have been outweighed by the marketing need for brand innovation. In general, straight-sided and two-point-contact bottles are easier to pack in multiples, so the outer packaging is usually simpler. Irregular packs are likely to need more outer packaging to help keep them upright in transit, so it is worth taking this into consideration when designing environmentally friendly packaging.

Shape can be extremely important when lightweighting packaging. For instance, sharp details and corners need to be avoided to allow an even flow of glass and prevent weak points. Alternatively, plastic bottles can benefit from additional detailing to improve rigidity when the wall thickness is reduced.

A distinctive shape is the best way to ensure a brand does not quickly reach its sell-by date. Orangina is an example of a drink that has a distinctive bottle shape which retains clear links to the original, even though the design evolved over many years. If it had been launched in a ring-pull can it might have disappeared into obscurity, but the bottle has given it the personality to keep it recognizable.

It can take just one major manufacturer investing in a new pack to shift the paradigm for an entire category.

Top-down sauce bottles (tottles) are an example of how this can lead to environmental benefits as well as functional improvements.

Inverting the bottles to spare consumers the time and inconvenience of squeezing, spooning or thumping them is not a difficult concept to grasp, and toiletries have been packed like this for many years. While several smaller companies introduced squeezable and top-down tomato ketchup bottles, Heinz initially tried to make a virtue, in their advertisements, of their glass bottles which had to be banged to release the sauce (because it is so thick) – as though inefficient packaging was an essential brand value. They eventually produced a squeezable bottle loosely based on the shape of their glass one. From this they developed the altogether more practical and distinctive top-down bottle they use today. In doing this, they boldly moved away from the classic sauce-bottle profile that had shaped their brand for many years in order to create a better, more relevant product with a smaller environmental footprint.

Simultaneously, other big brands, such as Hellman's Mayonnaise, recognized the value of making their products easier to use and developed their own distinctive inverted packs, helping them move their brands in a new direction. Although the caps are sometimes larger than they were (and are not necessarily recyclable), the packs themselves tend to have a larger capacity. They are certainly an improvement on the heavy, energy-hungry glass bottles they replace.

However, taking an environmental stance can risk the loss of a distinctive brand presence if it is not handled sensitively. Over the last few years almost all confectionery brands have moved to being sold in flow-wrap bags, mainly to control costs, increase shelf life and reduce materials, with the result that several previously distinctive brands have become anonymous. KitKat, for example, has lost the personality that came with the original paper and foil design as a result of developing more efficient packaging. Other internationally known confectionery brands that have clearly suffered a similar crisis include Toblerone, which is often packed in flow wrap, and Smarties, which have lost their iconic cardboard tube with its plastic top. Toblerone comes off better than most because its distinctive shape is still discernible, underlining the importance of ownability in physical branding.

Regrettably, from a branding standpoint, the future for sweets looks bag-shaped. From the perspective of cost and minimal use of materials, the environmental argument for flow wrap is watertight. However, there are some engaging physical formats, such as cans, that would allow ownability along with good recyclability so there is still room for innovation, despite the apparent limitations.

MODIFY A STANDARD PACK SHAPE

BRAND OWNERS ARE KEEN TO CREATE, AND WILL JEALOUSLY GUARD, DISTINCTIVE DESIGN ELEMENTS IN THEIR PACKAGING, BUT IF STANDARD MASS-PRODUCTION PACKAGING SYSTEMS, SUCH AS CANS, TINS AND DOY BAGS USE THE LEAST ENERGY OR ARE RECYCLABLE, CAN THEY EVER BE 'OWNED' BY A SINGLE BRAND?

Their efficiency is a given, but from the point of view of brand innovation they offer little opportunity unless the paradigm is shifted and they are used in a new way or for a product that is not normally packed using a given process.

The danger of this approach is that, although the new design may make an immediate impression, as soon as there are signs that the brand's market share is increasing competitors will be able to switch to the same type of pack without fear of infringing design rights.

There are a number of examples of companies that have created ownable packaging by using standard processes. Body Shop's Hemp range is such a case. Toiletries, normally packed in plastic injection or blow-moulded packs, were put into a variety of metal packs, including traditional shoe polish and lubricating oil tins, creating an engaging and ultimately award-winning range.

Gaultier took a similar route with can-packs for their fragrances. By being the first with such a radically different design they made their cans ownable in the fragrance category. The packs are copied from time to time, but there is no doubt who owns cans in the fragrance sector.

Fashion-related products like Gaultier's fragrances and the Hemp range have a head start in benefiting from paradigm-shifting packs. Because a playful innovative approach is often part of the brand, the designs are more a neat idea than an essential process.

Food is more of a challenge as filling-line speeds can be so fast that manufacturers usually depend on standard packaging systems, but here too there are examples of a process being owned by a single brand within a category. Gable-top cartons might seem to be the least likely format to spawn physical ownership, but this is what happened in the 1980s when the New Covent Garden Soup Company used a pack normally associated with milk and fruit juices to introduce their fresh soups. The packaging was a masterstroke; it immediately linked the soups with freshness and made them so successful that a whole new category was effectively created. Fresh soups are now

On the carton:

Open here

Milk cocktail
by Joe
Strawberry

Wheat Flour, Vegetable Oil(Palm Oil, Rapeseed, Soy and Corn Oil), Sugar, Lactose, Whole Milk Powder, Shortening, Butter, Salt, Dried Strawberry, Skim Milk Powder, Dextrin, Artificial Flavor(Strawberry and Milk), Red Beet Color, Soy Lecithin, Trisodium, Phosphate, Sodium Bicarbonate, Contains Milk, Wheat, and Soy

300 ml

Milk cocktail by Joe, designed by Studio Alex Hattomonkey

Above:
Tetrahedral tea bag

Below:
Innocent Tetra Pak

seen in a variety of pack formats in the United Kingdom, including plastic (polypropylene) tubs and pouches (doy bags), but despite competition from other brands as well as supermarket own-brands in gable-top packs, it is still the New Covent Garden Soup Company that is most identified with the format.

Another approach is to use the physical features of a pack to create a witty graphic look. The child-focused containers for milk cocktails, designed around the Batman character and a cow by the Russian Studio Alex Hattomonkey, are a good example, as is the banana juice pack by Naoto Fukasawa.

It is sometimes possible to adapt a process to create ownership. PG Tips tea bags and Phileas Fogg savoury snacks both came up with the same tetrahedral pack principle in different categories at about the same time. The flow-wrap tetrahedron, which is sometimes used for creamer packs, is created by taking a normal flow-wrapping machine of the type used for chocolate bar wrappers and adapting it by setting one set of sealing jaws at right angles to the other.

In practice the PG Tips tea bags became a runaway success, because the shape allows better circulation of the tea (or so the advertisement says), making it a better product, while although the Phileas Fogg snack bag was radical and engaging, its shape made it hard to control and orientate on-shelf, making it difficult to retail it effectively. The form follows function mantra applies to packaging, just as it does to any other three-dimensional design discipline. Innocent, makers of fresh smoothies, made use of a Tetra Wedge to create a distinctive triangular and recyclable 'tube' pack. This is simply a standard foil-lined Tetra Brik with the seal left to overhang rather than being folded against the sides of the pack. However, the use of space is inefficient compared to the conventional Tetra Brik, and is compounded by selling the smoothies as a multipack in an additional box.

FUNCTIONALITY

JUST AS SHAPE CAN DEFINE A PACK, SO CAN FUNCTIONALITY, PARTICULARLY WHEN VARIATIONS IN SHAPE ARE RESTRICTED. AEROSOL BRANDS ARE ALMOST AS RECOGNIZABLE BY THEIR TRIGGER DESIGN AS BY THEIR GRAPHICS. THIS WAS NOT ALWAYS THE CASE. FOR A LONG TIME, WHAT A PRODUCT LOOKED LIKE ON-SHELF WAS EVERYTHING, SO UNNECESSARILY TALL, SCULPTED OVERCAPS WERE THE NORM. THEY OFTEN CONCEALED STANDARD ATOMIZERS, SO ONCE A CAP WAS DISCARDED (AS IT INEVITABLY WAS) THERE WAS LITTLE PHYSICAL DIFFERENTIATION BETWEEN BRANDS.

Impulse aerosol spray can

Convenience – cat food in an aluminium tray

By the mid-1990s a few deodorant manufacturers had realized that exchanging the cap for a lockable trigger would not only create a more convenient product that could safely be carried in a handbag or sports bag, but would also achieve ownership through permanent physical branding. In Europe, Impulse were one of the first manufacturers to design a lockable cap format; today, many brands use ownable, locking sprayer designs to protect themselves from imitation by cheaper brands.

Other products where functionality is used to protect and enhance brands include cleaning products (such as toilet cleaners) and garden products (such as weedkillers). These often have some sort of unique dispenser that makes them more effective, easier to use and harder to copy, without necessarily having any more effect on the environment than a standard pack.

Functional differentiation – how a pack opens, whether it has a secondary function, an unusual texture or even a special sound – can be as important as sculptural form in defining a pack. For instance, a cube-shaped box of chocolates can be opened in a variety of ways that project different qualities about the contents: conventional, fashionable, innovative, practical, and so on.

Finding a way to improve the function of a pack rather than simply changing its shape is not only a more honest way of setting about a design. In practical terms, it is far easier to pitch to a client, because the pack's improved functionality clearly adds value to the product, whereas quantifying the largely subjective effect of a changed pack shape, simply 'because it looks better' can be less straightforward.

As discussed earlier, butter is often sold in tubs to create a more convenient rather than a superior product (see p. 18). Similarly, there are several reasons why cat food is sold in foil pouches. Manufacturers may argue that their shape is more space-efficient and that they are lighter than cans, and certainly the flat orientation makes the graphics more visible. But the major reason, as anyone who has washed up a can of cat food before putting it out for recycling soon realizes, is that squeezing the food out

of a disposable pouch is much more 'convenient' than washing out a foul-smelling can. The single-serving aluminium-tray pack bears this out. When it comes to washing the tray most of the cleaning has been done by the cat.

Pringles potato snacks are unusual in that they are uniquely shaped to be stacked efficiently into a cardboard tube. This differentiation from bagged crisps has been a key feature of their design since their launch. Times have moved on, though. Today, a dense foil-lined, non-recyclable cardboard tube with a resealable plastic lid has to be a questionable form of packaging in comparison to a lightweight bag. Pringles may counter that their packs are more efficient to transport than regular crisp bags. Their latest yogurt-style mini-packs are an interesting solution, with strong structural branding but reduced materials. The product's compact stacking format allows them to compete more effectively against the bagged competition.

However, when creating a functional pack it is always worth ensuring that environmental principles are not forgotten. For example, Gü, a premium dessert brand, produced an insulated container for ice cream. It was a fabulous idea, beautifully executed in black, expanded polystyrene with the logo moulded into it. But, of course, more than a logo is needed to sell food, so a card wrap was used for the pack graphics. Expanded polystyrene is not suitable for direct contact with ice cream, as it might be scooped out with the product. Better to put the ice cream in a plastic pot. But what if bits of polystyrene break away from the lid? The pot needs to be covered with greaseproof paper.

In this case the initial idea – an insulated container – led to a train of decisions which compounded the engaging, but already environmentally suspect, original concept, and ultimately created an expensive and unsustainable packaging solution. Gü continue to produce excellent desserts, beautifully packaged, but their ice-cream pack no longer graces retailers' shelves.

VINTAGE STYLING

BECAUSE OF A WIDESPREAD, IF MISGUIDED, PERCEPTION THAT PACKAGING WAS MORE SUSTAINABLE IN THE PAST, VINTAGE STYLING CAN BE USED TO CONVEY GREEN QUALITIES. FOR INSTANCE, SOAP MAY BE WRAPPED IN PAPER OR HAVE A TWINE BINDING WITH A SIMPLE PAPER TAG, CREATING A FRESH, HANDMADE IMAGE. SOME MANUFACTURERS MAKE A VIRTUE OF PRESENTING PRODUCTS, MADE AND WRAPPED BY HAND, THAT OFTEN HARK BACK TO THE PAST AND TO TRADITIONAL METHODS OF PRODUCTION.

The advantage of vintage styling over the more basic unbleached pulp and kraft style of packaging is that it does not preach, yet its message is no less clear. Hence, it is increasingly used to suggest traditional unadulterated quality and greener values, and often transcends niche categorization. Jordan's breakfast cereals, for example, have a strong typographic retro feel that suggests farm-fresh goodness and, by implication, greener packaging. In comparison, big-brand cereals struggle to convey any environmental message, despite using similar materials.

Retro packaging gives designers wider licence to experiment outside the narrow confines of what is normally perceived as environmentally friendly packaging, and can often be used for more contemporary products, particularly fashion brands, where it again makes the association between green and cool.

Traditional Japanese origata packaging uses natural materials and spans the boundary between vintage and grey-brown unbleached packaging. Beautiful and simple as it is, it tends not to lend itself to mass-market products, even in its home country – examples of environmentally friendly packaging are few and far between in Japan. Traditional packaging is sometimes mimicked by modern industrial processes to achieve the same look with modern standards of preservation, but in a far less sustainable format.

Vintage styling – retro packaging

LESS IS MORE

LESS IS MORE IS EASILY THE
MOST IMPORTANT RULE FOR
DESIGNING ENVIRONMENTALLY
FRIENDLY PACKAGING, BUT
ONE THAT IS ALL TOO EASILY
FORGOTTEN. PEOPLE TEND TO
FOCUS ON RECYCLING AS AN
ENVIRONMENTAL STRATEGY,
BUT IT IS FAR BETTER TO
USE LESS MATERIAL IN THE
FIRST PLACE.

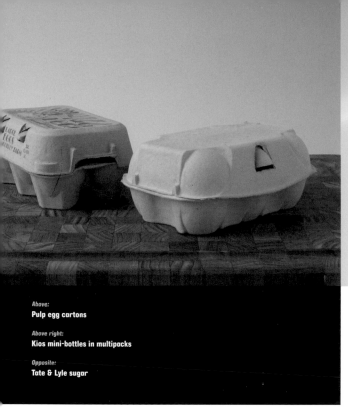

Some of the very best packs are the simplest. Remember butter before it was entombed in plastic? Egg boxes are simple and functional, yet new variations emerge from time to time so the design format is not entirely limiting. And there was once a time when it was possible to produce multipacks without the need for a full-length cardboard graphic wrap.

The function of each individual element in a pack should be considered. For example, if a pot of face cream has to be put in a carton to be sold, perhaps the pot should be designed differently. If a carton has a window, the designer should ask whether it needs film or could be left open, allowing the customer to touch the product. Leaving it open will not only use less material, but the packaging will cost less and be easier to recycle.

However, it can be the case that less is more – but not in a good way. The smaller a pack's volume, the larger its relative surface area. Mini-bottles and mini-cans seem particularly unnecessary. Convenience lunch-box products are a large market sector that falls into this category. As well as mini-bottles (sometimes with pull-spout closures), there are myriad mini-packs for biscuits and shrunken versions of other well-known products.

REDUCING THE CONTENT

As well as reducing the outer packaging, it is also possible to look at how the product it contains is dealt with in the first place. The strong movement towards concentrated detergents that wash at lower temperatures should theoretically result in less packaging, but this is not always the case. Concentrated laundry or dishwasher tablets, for instance, are certainly easier to use than powder, but they are usually individually wrapped. In all probability they are more eco-friendly than the larger and heavier unconcentrated versions, but the designer should consider whether the tablet is mainly a convenience format, which generates more packaging, when other dispensing solutions could be available.

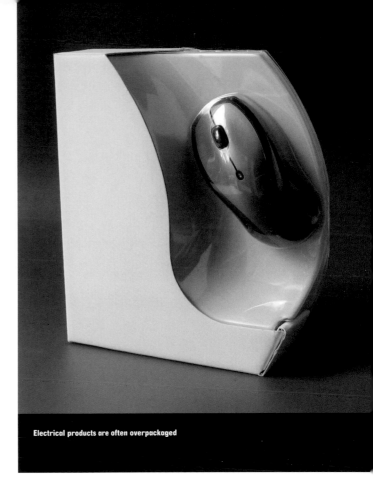

Electrical products are often overpackaged

REDUCING SPACE

Excess space around a product is another form of overpackaging. Apart from the sheer waste of energy involved in shipping air from place to place, it often amounts to little more than deception, especially when the product is not visible. Some of the worst offenders are electronic goods, computer software and, in particular, toys. When selling to children many companies seem to take the view that the larger and more impressive the packaging, the more desirable the product. To a certain extent they may be right, so designing environmentally friendly packs for toys can be a challenge.

Toy manufacturers like to show the whole product and, in the case of an action toy, put it in as dramatic and space-consuming a pose as possible – which often requires intricate wiring with plastic ties and copious amounts of cardboard. Accessories are usually shown, held in a separate vacuum forming or wired to the backboard rather than being hidden from view, which again takes up space.

Large, wrap-around windows that allow better product visibility are a common feature. Using a lightweight plastic for these would undermine the structure of the pack, so the answer is to use a thicker one. Folded clear plastic has inherent sculptural restrictions, so there has been a trend recently to use heavyweight vacuum formings to create huge, rounded windows, particularly for action figures and robotic toys.

Sifting through the layers of packaging, undoing the ties and separating out the plastic and graphic panels can be frustrating and time consuming. There is little that can be recycled, so it is hardly surprising that this type of packaging makes people angry.

The rule of thumb seems to be that 'fun' toys have exuberant, extravagant and thoroughly indefensible packaging, whereas 'educational' ones come in simple, practical, but usually unengaging carton board boxes and use openings rather than plastic windows. From a design point of view it is perfectly possible to find a creative middle ground, so that educational toys are more interesting and the fun ones more responsible.

With some rearranging the big-window toys can usually be put in smaller carton board boxes with smaller plastic windows (or openings). Avoiding complicated poses and large windows means there can be less plastic, fewer ties and a more efficient recyclable card structure. There is no need to show all the accessories, so concealing them in the box will also save space and materials.

If the environmental advantages are not clear to toy manufacturers the cost benefits are self-evident, but getting companies to reduce packaging can be a hard sell. When the market appears to dictate that packaging should be excessive simply to grab attention it is a brave manufacturer who will make the first move.

Not all toys are overpackaged. Although board games are sometimes overlarge, in general they are surprisingly restrained; they usually come in a rectangular box with a vacuum forming to hold loose items. If anything, board games are fertile ground for more interesting packaging, particularly in light of competition from video games.

Small appliances, electrical beauty products and audio products are often presented in high-visibility, welded vacuum formings, which in some ways are not dissimilar to toy packaging. Not only do they contain a great deal of single-use plastic; they also use clear plastic inserts and card graphic panels. In another common format a pair of nested, welded vacuum formings contains the product and frames it in a graphic carton, so that it appears to

CD jewel packaging

emerge from its box. This makes the packaging more manageable for shelf display, but uses an excessive amount of plastic inside a virtually empty box.

To some extent this type of packaging is intended to remove a potential buyer's need to inspect the product. A fully enclosed pack with a graphic image is often opened simply to check the product or its colour, making it unsaleable. Displaying products clearly means customers do not have to tamper with the packaging, and welding the blisters together physically prevents them doing so.

There are other ways to achieve the same ends. Many products can be exposed while being retained by the packaging. At its most basic this can mean using a window box with a retaining insert, but more sophisticated structures can be built around a product; the cardboard packaging often used for batteries is an example.

Even replacing a welded clam pack with a card-backed vacuum forming increases the potential for recycling.

Computer software is often packed in nondescript boxes several times larger than the DVD they contain, with little justification for their size other than perhaps making it more difficult for a shoplifter to conceal them. Many computer program manuals are on the DVD that carries the software, so most of the packaging is superfluous. It wastes not only materials, but also energy resources in shipping air. In essence, the large impressive box goes some way to justifying the price for its uninspiring contents, but not much else.

One would not expect to buy a DVD in anything other than a case, which protects the disc (special editions excluded), so it is surprising that software is so blatantly overpackaged. Although the computer industry usually offers it in downloadable form, many people still prefer the reassurance of buying software on disc – but a computer program does not have to be in a box five times larger

than a DVD. It could further be argued that a DVD case does not need to be any larger than a CD case.

The digital revolution has made one packaging format an endangered species. The music industry is booming but CD sales are in freefall, such is the dominance of downloadable music formats like iTunes and MP3. The CD jewel case has never really been an entirely satisfactory format. Easily broken or cracked, it never generated the visual excitement or graphic adaptability of its forerunner, the LP sleeve.

Cameras are packaged primarily with protection in mind, but mobile phones, which are more teen- and fashion-related, tend to have a playful element, which leads to more interesting packs, but also to more materials.

Some larger retailers are beginning to put pressure on their suppliers to reduce their packaging and Amazon, in particular, are insisting on smaller packs for mailing. This is much more likely to work than a self-regulating approach, as it creates genuine pressure to conform.

The Internet mail-order format should itself make presentation less important. A product has to compete only with other products in a photograph, so while the pack should always be engaging there is no need for it to be excessive. Smaller packs are clearly better all round, but using pulp or recycled paper to replace vacuum formings adds weight. This means that, as well as balancing the environmental cost of the extra weight versus material choice, outside factors like additional postage costs need to be considered as part of the mix.

Blander outer packaging suited to mail order has led some manufacturers to place more emphasis on the 'out of box experience' (OOBE), ostensibly to enrich and simplify the process of unwrapping and installing a new product. Some, such as Apple, manage to create beautiful,

minimal packs which complement their products. However, there is a danger that by creating unnecessary sequential component layouts that lead the customer step by step through the installation and assembly of an electronic gadget, manufacturers generate far more packaging than there would be if the various parts were simply properly labelled within a smaller box. Generating added value through OOBE is fast becoming the norm and this approach could become self-perpetuating as manufacturers vie for market share.

Shelf ready packaging, which effectively turns the outer carton into an on-shelf dispenser, is extremely popular with retailers. It means the product does not have to be arranged and constantly dressed, making the job of shelf-stacking much easier and helping to reduce staff costs. However, products that were once packed to fill a transit carton as tightly and efficiently as possible have to be oriented in an upright front-facing position, ready for merchandising. This can reduce the number of packs in an outer carton by as much as 50 per cent, so there is a great deal of potential for wasting energy in transportation and packaging materials.

LIGHTWEIGHTING

MUCH OF THE DEVELOPMENT IN ENVIRONMENTAL PACKAGING SOLUTIONS IS NOW BASED ON STRAIGHTFORWARD WEIGHT REDUCTION. THIS IS LEADING TO SOME EXTREMELY EFFICIENT, BUT RATHER AUSTERE RESULTS. HARDLY SURPRISING GIVEN THE INVESTMENT THAT HAS ALREADY BEEN PLOUGHED INTO EXISTING PROCESSES AND THE NEED FOR MEASURABLE IMPROVEMENTS TO MEET GOVERNMENT TARGETS IN WASTE REDUCTION.

Reducing the pack weight not only uses the raw material more efficiently, but also reduces the amount of energy it takes to move the product from place to place. In so doing, it also reduces the cost. Therefore, a great deal of industry effort is currently focused on lightweighting materials, whether they be plastics, card, glass or metal. This is especially true of glass, which is particularly dense and heavy. Cans for drinks have been developed to have walls no thicker than a human hair and carton board is available in a wide range of lightweighted formats.

There is often a choice of alternative substrates. For instance, glass bottles for soft drinks have, to a large extent, been supplanted by PET, which has reduced transport and production emissions, now with the additional bonus that PET is readily recyclable.

Doy bags or pouches are a lightweight alternative to a variety of pack formats, including cans, foil-sealed trays, injection-moulded tubs and beverage cartons. While they are not usually recyclable their weight, space efficiency and ease of manufacture are alternative environmental advantages.

The table on page 112 from INCPEN shows how the typical weight of some familiar packs has changed over the years.

Above:
Modern aluminium drink can – no seam and walls that are thinner than human hair

Opposite:
Thick-walled and seamed 1970s steel drink can

PACKAGING REDUCTION EXAMPLES	1950s	1960s	1970s	1990s	2000	2008	% change
Washing-up liquid bottle (1 litre)			120 g	67 g	50 g	43 g	64%
Soup can (400 g)	90 g		69 g	57 g	55 g	49 g	46%
Yogurt pot		12 g	7 g	5 g		4 g	67%
Plastics fizzy drinks bottle (2 litres)			58 g		43 g	40 g	31%
Metal drinks can (300 ml)		60 g		21 g	15 g	14 g	77%
Glass beer bottle (275 g)			450 g		325 g	176 g	61%
Glass milk bottle (1 pint)	538 g		397 g	230 g		186 g	65%

In the film *Jaws* there is a good example of how packaging materials have been reduced since the 1970s. Quint, grizzled captain of the fishing boat *Orca* that was chartered to find the shark, finishes his can of beer and crushes it with one hand. The oceanographer mocks this macho display, and sarcastically crushes his paper cup in response. In 1974, when *Jaws* was filmed, beer cans used approximately four times the material of today's cans. Now beer cans are engineered to have the minimum wall thickness that ensures their functionality, and anyone can be a Quint.

Lightweighting suits many manufacturers because it can allow them to carry on running their products without changing their packaging processes or, perhaps more importantly, altering the look of their packs. Successful brands are hard won, so manufacturers may view major changes with suspicion, but lightweighting allows them to comply with government environmental legislation while benefiting from savings in transport and material costs.

The difficulty with lightweighting is that, because the end product often looks the same as the original one, it is not always clear that anything has been changed. Given the goodwill a greener product can generate, this can be frustrating for manufacturers, and they often lavish significant effort in generating the public relations to make up the shortfall.

Some global brands have been extremely proactive in this way. Coca-Cola, for instance, have – with a fair amount of razzamatazz – produced lightweight versions of their iconic glass bottles that use 20 per cent less material, and also designed new aluminium and PET bottles. By keeping the shape of the bottle they have retained Coke's status as the most recognized beverage brand worldwide, whereas Pepsi Cola, their arch competitor, could be said to suffer from the lack of a consistent pack format. Coca-Cola have even reduced the volume of their concentrate so that it can be shipped more efficiently. They experiment constantly with more sustainable packaging for their brands, and have invested heavily in high-visibility recycling schemes.

BRAND DEVELOPMENT

Carte Noire premium instant coffee provides an interesting example of how a brand can develop while improving its environmental profile. In the early 1990s it was well known and popular in France, but far too overpackaged and costly to be suitable for wider distribution. A plastic lid covered the top half of the jar and a base moulding covered the bottom third. Each of these had shrink-sleeved graphics, which left only a small section of the jar uncovered by plastic. The solution was to retain the Art Deco look of the packaging, remove the base moulding and drastically reduce the size of the lid, while incorporating a premium-feel embossed emblem on the lid.

Carte Noire has been redesigned once again and, although the changes are more cosmetic than they were in the previous incarnation, the lid now has a flat top that allows it to stack, which not only makes it easier to handle in the supermarket, but also means there is no need for a spacer between layers when the jars are packed in a carton. There is still scope to reduce the size of the lid further and lightweight the glass, so perhaps this will happen the next time the brand is updated.

Original Carte Noire jar

Modern design solution retaining brand essence

Latest design evolution

USE RECYCLABLE MATERIALS

RECYCLING IS CLEARLY AN EXTREMELY IMPORTANT WAY OF REDUCING OUR CARBON FOOTPRINT, BUT LOCAL CLOSED-LOOP RECYCLING IS MUCH BETTER THAN WHAT IS OFTEN CALLED DOWNCYCLING – SENDING MATERIALS LONG DISTANCES TO BE REPROCESSED INTO LOW-GRADE PRODUCTS AND MATERIALS.

The easiest materials to sort and reprocess usefully are aluminium, steel, clear PET, clear HDPE, glass, paper, card and moulded pulp. All plastics are theoretically recyclable, but it is simply not economically or environmentally efficient to collect or separate many of them, so the list varies from country to country and region to region.

However, recycling is developing quickly, as new technologies automate many of the processes previously done by hand and make sorting faster and more accurate. Crucially, there is a growing market for recycled materials, and efficient collection and reprocessing have done much to reduce their cost.

Colour, or lack of it, is an essential element in designing recyclable plastic packs: coloured recyclate is extremely difficult to reprocess with any degree of colour accuracy, so often ends up in low-grade applications, such as garden furniture, insulation or synthetic lumber. This certainly does nothing to reduce the amount of bottles produced from virgin plastic. Food-grade closed-loop recycling plants for reprocessing PET and HDPE concentrate on clear plastics, as they are the most abundant and consistent, and are the easiest to identify.

One of the areas where manufacturers have made a positive contribution to plastics recovery has been through colouring the product rather than the packaging, making it more attractive by using special effects, such as bubbles, speckles and pearlescence. Clear packs can easily be usefully and efficiently recycled.

Even as recycling becomes still more efficient, making it easier to sort more materials, colour will probably remain a limiting factor, so if materials such as PP and PS are more widely collected the best environmental choice for designers would always be the material's 'default' colour.

High-profile green packaging is based, almost without exception, on unbleached paper and pulp, as this is what many people expect from environmentally friendly packaging. Packs made from these materials, or card, can be better for the environment than other ones. They use fewer chemicals and avoid clay coatings, which add to the residue when paper products are processed and reprocessed as part of recycling.

Traditionally, brown paper and pulp were associated with the most basic types of everyday staple, but they have come to represent much more than this. To expand on an earlier example, the appeal of buying meat, bagged and bloody, from a butcher, or cereal loose from a health-food store is that doing so makes an anti-brand statement about seeking genuine product quality. And therein lies a clue to some high-profile environmentally friendly packs. Recycled pulp and natural-fibre packaging often picks up on these clues. It says: 'I care about the important things. Quality, sustainability, consideration for others, so I don't mind paying more.' In reality, this is often another form of branding. The challenge for the designer is to make the packaging as sustainable as it appears to be, otherwise the process becomes either well-meant folly or an exercise in unalloyed cynicism.

Overtly 'green' packs can appear to be rather worthy, alternative luxury products, which often puts off people making day-to-day purchases, so this type of packaging tends to be used for niche products rather than mainstream ones. Websites and labelling for high-visibility green products can be informal and amusing, even iconoclastic, yet this creativity seldom extends to the packs.

Curiously, designers of look-at-me green packaging seem to have an almost evangelical need to incorporate seeds in their packs, so that they can be buried and start absorbing carbon dioxide without a moment to lose. This is very symbolic, but it actually lessens the likelihood that the packs can be recycled, and they will almost certainly never be planted.

The advantages of using many of the 'unprocessed' overtly green materials are debatable, particularly if their poor print finish leads, as it often does, to stickers being used for graphics. Recycled board also needs to be, quite literally, weighed up against lightweighted board, which has other environmental advantages. In the mainstream, recycled-content paper board and basic brown kraft cartons with a white facing layer for printing have become commonplace, and are practical environmental solutions.

Bioplastics are currently overhyped as sustainable materials but can make a contribution; in particular, they can be used to replace hard-to-recycle packaging materials, such as plastic films. Confectionery is an area where they have an opportunity to shine. Some retailers have introduced chocolates in packs that feature compostable, water-soluble trays which, unlike many other bioplastics, biodegrade quickly. Bioplastics are not currently as recyclable as other materials. Innocent, the environmentally conscious, ethical manufacturer of fruit smoothies, fell foul of the hype when they trialled a PLA (bioplastic) bottle in 2007 with the aim of using fewer fossil plastics, claiming controversially that the material was carbon neutral. They soon realized they had created a monster that was not only non-recyclable but was also non-compostable within the prevailing infrastructure. So, after a few months and some negative publicity, they withdrew the bottle and replaced it with what was billed as the world's first plastic bottle that used 100 per cent recycled PET. Innocent subsequently found that the quality and colour consistency of rPET has declined over the years, giving a heavily tinted appearance to some of their lighter smoothies and making them look less appetizing. So they have temporarily reduced the rPET content to a more manageable 35 per cent. They are working with their suppliers to produce cleaner grades of rPET, so they can increase the recycled content again.

Using materials when there is no realistic chance they will achieve their environmental potential only helps to create additional landfill waste. For instance, compostable and biodegradable materials are not necessarily home compostable; in order to break down they usually have to be sent to industrial composting facilities where they can be exposed to heat and additional moisture. Some materials, particularly bioplastics, may not degrade within the statutory composting time frame, even if they are accepted for composting. The message, therefore, is that where possible designers should choose the most widely recycled materials, which can be reprocessed locally, so that there is a realistic chance they will be recycled without running up too many additional carbon miles.

Paperfoam, an innovative injection-mouldable starch-based material, is a good example of how bioplastics can be used effectively. It is recyclable with paper and compostable, and is often used as a distinctive high-quality alternative to vacuum formings in transit packaging and bioplastic CD cases.

MATERIALS SHOULD BE EASY TO SEPARATE

Designers should look at how easily materials can be separated for recycling. How much work will this involve for the consumer or recyling plant? Multilayer materials are especially difficult to recycle. Drinks cartons are recoverable, but the practicality and effectiveness of this form of recycling is debatable, especially since it is, to a large extent, underwritten by carton manufacturers, who have the most to lose from the perception that they are selling an environmentally unfriendly product.

Features such as staples and firmly glued windows make card more difficult to recycle. Even effects such as holographic and other printing processes on card usually require plastic lamination, which makes the pack harder to recycle.

Labels and sleeves should be easily removable. For instance, if PVC sleeves are not properly removed from PET bottles they can seriously contaminate and weaken the recycled material. Better still: do not use PVC.

Paperfoam moulded tray

117

USE RECYCLED MATERIALS

MORE AND MORE RECYCLED MATERIALS ARE BECOMING AVAILABLE AS THE RECYCLING INDUSTRY DEVELOPS. RPET AND RHDPE MAKE IT POSSIBLE TO CHOOSE RECYCLED FOOD-GRADE PLASTICS THAT CAN BE USED EITHER WHOLE OR BLENDED WITH VIRGIN PLASTICS. THEY ARE PARTICULARLY SOUGHT AFTER BY MANUFACTURERS AND RETAILERS WHO ARE SEEKING TO IMPROVE THE ENVIRONMENTAL PROFILE OF THEIR PLASTIC PACKAGING, AND THEREFORE THEY CAN ATTRACT A HIGH PREMIUM.

McDonald's packaging from France

Glass, steel, aluminium, paper, card and pulp packaging all have the potential to use recycled material in their manufacture. Aluminium, in particular, is recycled effectively, and the recyclate uses 95 per cent less energy than virgin aluminium. Most aluminium cans contain a proportion of recycled material – in Europe, this is around 50 per cent of the content.

Card and paper products are typically derived from trees or cotton, which are usually farmed as crops, so they have the additional advantage of being sustainable as well as recyclable. The advantages of using recycled but relatively heavy card have to be balanced against those of lightweighted board, which uses less energy in transit.

McDonald's have visibly greened up their packaging, replacing their styrofoam cartons with printed cardboard ones that use 72 per cent recycled paper. Not only does this make use of renewable and largely recycled materials, but the carton's structure means it requires significantly

less storage space, while the high-definition printing improves the impression of quality. Is it recyclable? Card that comes into contact with food generally cannot be recycled, but the carton's biodegradability, combined with better use of materials, certainly makes it an improvement on the original, and contributes to McDonald's corporate environmental strategy, which includes reducing plastics and recycling cooking oil as biodiesel.

Newton make running shoes and are an example of a manufacturer who is seeking to navigate a realistic route between pulp and recycled card. They produced a pulp-based, compact shoebox with the intention of using more environmentally friendly materials and saving space during transportation. Or so it would seem. After generating a great deal of interest and publicity the shoebox proved to be more costly to produce and less environmentally friendly to ship than Newton's existing packaging. This was partly because of the pulp manufacturer's distance from the shoe factory, but also because the box did not stack efficiently in transit. It is questionable whether the compact design saved any space at all since it created an irregular shape, which means the shipping container would carry a lot of air, rather than extra shoes.

Newton were forced to redesign the box more conventionally in order to achieve a better environmental profile. Instead of the distinctive pulp tray, they opted for a standard rectangular box, using consumer-recycled card and soy-based inks. While this appears to be a victory for common sense it might be argued that the pulp tray could have been made more practical, and the standard carton could have been more engaging. It seems that Newton ultimately achieved an environmentally friendly solution that they were comfortable with while generating a significant amount of goodwill, not to mention favourable press coverage.

Above:
Newton running shoes packaging before

Left:
Newton running shoes packaging after

CREATIVE, COOL AND GREEN

Method household cleaning products are a good example of creatively driven greener packaging. They use brightly coloured liquid products and more responsible materials, typically post-consumer recycled PET, combined with interesting pack structures. In effect, Method promote environmentally motivated choices as being engaging and cool, rather than drab and dutiful.

Despite the environmental message, Method's ranges have tended to feature a significant number of trigger packs and pumps with surprisingly few refill options. But their recent pump pack for dishwashing liquid is strongly marketed with reuse in mind. They have also been willing to experiment with sustainable materials, such as the perhaps extravagant, but nonetheless beautiful, bamboo-pulp packaging for its now discontinued Omop range refills. Their packaging policy is pragmatic and straightforward; clear, post-consumer recycled and recyclable materials are used where possible. They have avoided falling into the trap of using PLA bioplastic which, they explain, can contaminate the recycling stream and does not compost effectively.

In their watershed ranges Method have managed to associate creative pack design with greener trading; and while their products may not yet be entirely mainstream they certainly dominate a sizeable and expanding niche hitherto occupied by less attractive, eco-message-heavy brands.

SPECIFY LOCALLY AVAILABLE MATERIAL

It is important to distinguish between locally produced materials and ones that have acquired a significantly higher carbon footprint because they are transported from a different continent. Packaging materials are sometimes not readily available in the country where a product is manufactured. For instance, Bagasse, sugar-cane residue that can be pulped and moulded to form a better surface than traditional wood-pulp mouldings, often has to be transported from South America or Asia for use in Europe. Choosing to use it would be open to question when other pulp products are available locally. The same applies to specifying recycled materials. If rPET for use in the United States comes all the way from East Asia its environmental credentials will be somewhat tarnished. Most consumers and many retailers do not look beyond the 'recycled' label – and they should not have to do so.

DESIGN WITH REUSE IN MIND

SOME FORMS OF PACKAGING LEND THEMSELVES TO REUSE EITHER BY THE CONSUMER, PERHAPS WITH REFILLS, OR THROUGH A DEPOSIT-BASED BOTTLE COLLECTION SCHEME. SEVERAL NORTHERN EUROPEAN COUNTRIES RECYCLE BOTH GLASS AND PET BOTTLES THAT ARE GENERICALLY DESIGNED AND CAN BE RELABELLED BY DIFFERENT MANUFACTURERS. DESPITE THEIR ADDITIONAL WEIGHT, SUCH MULTITRIP CONTAINERS HAVE A SIGNIFICANTLY BETTER CARBON FOOTPRINT THAN RECYCLED BOTTLES: SOME HAVE THE POTENTIAL TO BE REUSED UP TO 30 TIMES.

Refill packs are underexploited; their success over the years has been patchy and, some would say, they are difficult to market as a result. But there are signs that they are becoming more widely accepted by consumers. They offer the potential to reduce material use significantly, but are necessarily less convenient than primary packs, although some function adequately without the need to transfer the contents.

To some extent manufacturers may believe that refills are not in their best interest, as they potentially detract from the added value of a custom pack and create potential imbalances of supply when only refills are available in-store and not the primary pack. Nevertheless, there are signs that consumers are warming to them. In all likelihood, even if the big brands do not show much interest in refills, it would not be surprising if supermarket own-brands and specialist suppliers expanded their offers in this area, with exclusive refill ranges.

In the United Kingdom Kenco have made commercial capital out of their eco-refill packs. The packs are 97 per cent lighter than their glass jars and, importantly, Kenco make this a key feature of their advertisements (although they say 97 per cent less packaging). They have stolen a march on their competitors and, if their competitors respond in kind, created a new market segment for coffee, perhaps boosting the potential for spin-off refill packs in other retail sectors.

As with recycling, a great deal of the success of refills is down to how the system is managed. The Body Shop experimented with allowing customers to bring back empty toiletry bottles and refill them in-store for a reduced price. The take-up was too small to make the system practical (around 1 per cent), but some niche stores, such as Unpackaged, specialize in selling unpackaged goods. For conventional shops and supermarkets, this approach is over-reliant on the goodwill of the customer – first to bring back empties and second to be bothered to fill, seal and label what they have bought. And for the supermarkets there would be little incentive for this type of scheme, apart from a reflected feel-good factor. It would require investment, organization and dedicated staff to help customers and mop up spills. On the other hand, they would be able to blame their customers if the scheme failed to generate any interest.

A far better way to deal with refills is to use minimal packaging, sold in the same size as the primary pack, so that all the contents can be decanted in one go. There is an argument that refills should allow customers to use the

Kenco refill

product and reseal the pack, even though this might be in a less convenient format than the primary pack. This has some merit, but tends to restrict refills to products that can easily be used and resealed. The most efficient way to save materials is a non-resealable lightweight bag, potentially with some sort of integral funnel to aid decanting.

Refills could be of particular benefit for the type of pack that has a mechanical dispenser which is normally discarded when the rest of the pack is recycled. Liquid soap is probably the most successful example of this, but there is little reason why many other pump products should not be catered for with refills. These could include window, bathroom and kitchen cleaners, and even pumped toiletries such as moisturizers and gels. But why stop at pumps? Roll-on deodorants, like spray window cleaners when they were first introduced, were commonly sold as refills, but are now almost always for single use.

Despite their small size there is a grotesque amount of packaging relative to the product.

While designers do not always have the option of designing refills to accompany the primary packaging, they can help facilitate their use. Trigger sprays and pump pots should have screw fittings, rather than snap-on fittings which are hard to remove. Narrow neck openings also restrict refilling. The refills themselves need to fulfil the minimum function of transferring their contents smoothly and easily to the primary pack, without spillage, otherwise they may not be purchased a second time.

GOOD ENVIRONMENTAL LABELLING

AFTER DESIGNING A PACK WITH GOOD GREEN CREDENTIALS IT IS IMPORTANT TO LABEL IT CORRECTLY. THE AMOUNT AND VARIETY OF INFORMATION ON PACKAGING CAN BE BEWILDERING, AND ENVIRONMENTAL LABELLING SHOULD BE PRESENTED CLEARLY AND ABUNDANTLY. IT DOES NOT ONLY INFORM THE CUSTOMER, IT CAN ALSO BE AN ESSENTIAL TOOL FOR DEMONSTRATING THE RETAILER/MANUFACTURER'S ENVIRONMENTAL COMMITMENT. THE DANGER IS THAT IT CAN BE USED SIMPLY AS A VEHICLE FOR PRESENTING A COMPANY IN AN ENVIRONMENTALLY FRIENDLY LIGHT WITHOUT GIVING THE CUSTOMER MUCH MEANINGFUL INFORMATION.

Environmental symbols for packaging

Good labelling is important as it describes a pack's environmental impact, but it is essential to be sure of the facts. There are an increasing number of independent organizations, not to mention industry competitors, who will challenge meaningless, misleading and downright false claims for products.

It is useful for consumers to know what the pack materials are, and whether:
- the pack can be recycled
- the pack is compostable
- the materials are biodegradable
- the materials are recycled
- the pack has been lightweighted to save energy and materials
- the pack size has been reduced to save energy and materials
- If possible, recycling information should be included on all packaging elements that can be recycled

Consumers generally recognize independent environmental attainment symbols such as the Forest Stewardship Council logo, but there are so many of them that they can be confusing. Manufacturers' and retailers' own environmental symbols carry very little weight and could well be branded as greenwash (see p 130) by environmental groups.

Non-committal recycling notices that refer consumers to their local authority for recycling information are unhelpful, but perhaps inevitable because of the piecemeal recycling facilities most countries operate. International brands that use the same pack in countries with different recycling systems face a similar situation. In these cases it is important to clearly identify the pack materials.

Some environmental labelling systems give carbon-emission figures. These are useful in theory, but for the average consumer, who is unable to compare them with those of similar products, they are probably meaningless. However, it is interesting that the packaging and disposal elements of a product often seem to be small in relation to its overall carbon emissions.

DO NOT MISLEAD THE CONSUMER

Not all recyclable materials are widely recycled, so it is disingenuous to be less than specific. Plastic-recycling symbols can give the impression that a specific plastic is widely recyclable, but many plastics are not routinely collected for a variety of reasons. These include low efficiency (it is simply not worth expending the energy needed to collect, clean and reprocess them), contamination or that they are not available in quantities that would make collecting them viable.

Materials that give an impression of sustainability are often used when nothing could be further from the truth. Grainy paper laminated to aluminium foil is an example, or the fibrous trays sometimes used for premium, organic cooked meat.

Making false or exaggerated environmental claims for a product – greenwashing – is a growth industry, and, with several websites devoted to the subject, consumers are becoming more aware of it. Definitions of environmentally friendly packaging are often vague and easily exploited, so accusations of greenwash are not difficult to find.

Some environmental groups have published their definitions of greenwash. Perhaps the most comprehensive is '10 signs of Greenwash' by Futerra, which contains good advice for both designers and specifiers. They were drawn up in response to excessive claims by advertisers, but could equally well apply to packaging.

10 SIGNS OF GREENWASH

1.	**Fluffy language**	*Words or terms with no clear meaning; for example, eco-friendly.*
2.	**Green products v dirty company**	*For example, energy-efficient light bulbs made in a factory that pollutes rivers.*
3.	**Suggestive pictures**	*Green images that indicate a (unjustified) green impact; for example, flowers blooming in exhaust pipes.*
4.	**Irrelevant claims**	*Emphasizing one tiny, green attribute when everything else is un-green.*
5.	**Best in class?**	*Declaring a product is slightly greener than the rest, even if the rest are pretty terrible.*
6.	**Just not credible**	*Eco-friendly cigarettes anyone? Greening a dangerous product doesn't make it safe.*
7.	**Gobbledygook**	*Jargon and information that only a scientist could check or understand.*
8.	**Imaginary friends**	*A label that looks like third-party endorsement ... except it's made up.*
9.	**No proof**	*It could be right, but where's the evidence?*
10.	**Outright lying**	*Totally fabricated claims or data.*

As the marketing benefits of taking an environmentally friendly approach become apparent to manufacturers it is clear that some of them prefer to create the impression of commitment, rather than making genuine changes to their products. Often, this is simply because of a lack of understanding about environmental processes rather than a wilful desire to deceive. Certainly, the level of suspicion shown by some environmental groups to big business in general is hardly warranted; their disappointment when it was revealed how low Coca-Cola's carbon footprint was (when compared to Innocent fruit smoothies) was palpable. Based on the whole product, the suggestion was that Coca-Cola emitted in the region of 25 per cent less carbon dioxide than Innocent; yet based on packaging alone Innocent had a slightly better footprint.

Current examples of greenwash being applied to packaging might include environmentally friendly, concentrated, low-temperature washing liquid with an overlarge cap and dispenser; or a hand soap-dispenser that makes a feature of using recycled PET, but has an extremely large, non-recyclable pump and no prospect of refills.

One much-publicized and supposedly green detergent pack replaced a recyclable, refillable bottle with a non-recyclable bag and press-button tap in a recyclable carton board box, like a wine box. Nice thinking, but not necessarily much of an advance.

Then there is the compostable water bottle which, apart from being a single-use container for a lifestyle product that is readily available from a tap, uses PLA bioplastic grown from corn. It is not really compostable, probably contains genetically modified corn and, if recycled accidentally, will contaminate the recycling stream rendering any recyclate unusable.

PLA is aggressively marketed and widely perceived to be a green material, but within the packaging industry many are sceptical of its benefits.

Similar controversy applies to oxo-biodegradable plastics (used for biodegradable carrier bags). Whether the plastic is actually digested by microbes or simply broken into very small pieces remains a subject of intense debate.

Biofuels and, by association, bioplastics have frequently been attacked as having a poorer environmental profile than the one they like to project, but the possibility that some of the controversy has been generated by those with most to lose if they gain a toehold – namely oil producers – cannot be entirely ruled out.

Emphasizing a product's good points is a key part of marketing, so it is often difficult to establish at which point this becomes greenwash. Glass manufacturers are not going to point out how heavy glass is compared with plastic. Manufacturers of plastic bottles will not reveal that if a bottle is recycled it may travel from the West to the Far East for reprocessing. Similarly, aluminium producers will stress how little energy it takes to recycle their product, rather than how much it takes to produce it in the first place.

Terra Choice, an American environmental marketing firm, points out that the total number of products making green claims increased by approximately 79 per cent in stores they visited in 2007 and 2008. Although there is legislation concerning green labelling there are so many different systems to convey the relative greenness of a product that they can be confusing. To some extent this plays into the hands of those who want to put an environmental gloss on their not-so-environmental products.

Campaigners argue that the whole issue of greenwash needs to be properly addressed, as it affects the credibility of green products in general. If environmental claims are routinely greeted with cynicism the public's perceptions of sustainability will be damaged and genuinely green products will be lost in the melée.

KEEP UP TO DATE

WHAT IS ENVIRONMENTALLY UNFRIENDLY TODAY, MAY NOT NECESSARILY BE ENVIRONMENTALLY UNFRIENDLY TOMORROW. THIS APPLIES PARTICULARLY TO THE RAPIDLY EVOLVING AREA OF RECYCLING, WHERE THE EXPLOSION OF RECOVERY TECHNOLOGIES, AND IMPROVEMENTS TO THE INFRASTRUCTURE FOR COLLECTING MATERIALS ARE SET TO MAKE LIFE EASIER, NOT ONLY FOR CREATIVES WITH A GREEN AGENDA, BUT ALSO RETAILERS AND MANUFACTURERS STRUGGLING TO COMPLY WITH GOVERNMENT GREEN INITIATIVES, WHICH ARE OFTEN BASED ON RECOVERY RATES.

As with new 'sustainable' materials, advances in recycling need to be treated with a little caution. Despite public perception, recycling is still the inferior option to reducing pack materials.

Composting processes, too, are overdue for widespread development. The dawning realization that vast quantities of food waste are simply being dumped in landfill sites to release methane could be the catalyst that leads to more widespread and effective use of composting as a means of disposal. Anaerobic digestion, in particular, is an efficient way of disposing of biodegradable packaging which may not degrade using conventional methods, yet, currently, packaging of any sort is often not accepted for composting.

Bioplastics currently lag behind conventional plastics in terms of performance, but are becoming more refined, with better barrier and sealing properties. More flexible composting facilities could go a long way to improving their environmental profile. Improvements in capturing methane from landfill (aimed mainly at exploiting emissions from food waste) will make a significant difference to the environmental profile of bioplastics and other biodegradable materials, such as paper and card, even when they are not recycled or composted.

Perhaps the most progress will come from continued materials reduction and innovation. For instance, recent encouraging developments have started to address the presentation of raw meat, which is usually packed in heat-sealed plastic or aluminium trays. Lately, large cuts of meat are more often shrink-wrapped and, despite the mildly detrimental effect this has on their appearance, it drastically reduces the volume and weight of packaging materials. The presentation issue has been successfully addressed by an innovative packaging system that uses inflated, gas-flushed bags to achieve the same effect as tray-based packs. In this case, the environmental argument is forcefully backed up by the potential cost savings of a bag-based system.

COCA-COLA LIGHTWEIGHT GLASS BOTTLE

Coca-Cola have been quicker than most companies to recognize the importance of presenting a more environmentally responsible image to consumers, perhaps mindful of how global brands (such as McDonald's) can be undermined by complacency. Their massive output and high profile make them an easy target for environmental groups, so a rolling programme of packaging reduction addresses some of the campaigners' concerns while enhancing he product's image.

The classic Contour glass bottle most people associate with Coke has had a chequered recent history. It was briefly replaced by a straight-sided bottle in the 1970s, and later came under threat from cheaper and lighter PET bottles – so there was good reason to design a more lightweight glass bottle. The Ultra is 20 per cent lighter than the Contour, 40 per cent stronger and 10 per cent cheaper to produce. Although it is slightly dumpier than the original it retains much of its spirit, and even emphasizes the curves that have always made the bottle so distinctive.

Like Tetra Pak, Coca-Cola have committed substantial resources to developing reprocessing facilities. They have constructed the world's largest PET closed-loop (bottle to bottle) recycling plant at Spartanburg, South Carolina, with a capacity of 100 million pounds of recycled PET per annum, enough to mould 2 billion 20-ounce bottles.

More recently they have been developing the Plantbottle, a PET bottle that contains 30 per cent bio-based plastic derived from sugar cane. Unlike biodegradable bioplastics, this is based on a process that converts bio-ethanol to conventional plastics, so the bottle retains all the characteristics of fossil plastics and, unlike PLA bottles, can be recycled in the normal way.

Above and opposite:
Iconic Coca-Cola bottles

HELP REMEDIES

Help Remedies is a range of pills and first-aid products with a distinctly user-friendly feel. Its developers, Richard Fine and Nathan Frank, both of whom have advertising backgrounds, took standard healthcare remedies based on tried and trusted ingredients, such as aspirin and ibuprofen, which are normally marketed in reassuringly clinical packaging, and rebranded them in the more approachable style of homeopathic products.

The packaging is mainly based on locally sourced paper pulp and bioplastic, and is clearly environmentally friendly. However, it avoids falling into the trap of using unbleached pulp and low-quality mouldings, so manages to transcend the 'worthy' niche, and simply becomes excellent packaging.

Its beauty is that it does not exist in a vacuum, as a token environmentally friendly product, but is a key building block of an extremely sophisticated brand. It encompasses ethical principles (of course), witty advertising, a simple but informative website, attractive point-of-sale units and even a range of must-have Help T-shirts. The tone of voice is in the same casual vein as Ben & Jerry's or Innocent smoothies but this does not erode the impression that Help provide effective healthcare products.

The pack has evolved from a simple, card-sealed pulp moulding with a rip-strip opening to a resealable pulp case that features a colour-coded bioplastic band. Its biodegradability is a key feature, but the proof of a pudding is in the eating so a web page is devoted to monitoring a pack as it breaks down over a period of several days. It even charts the clear lack of biodegradability displayed by the PLA. While the use of bioplastic might be challenged, and the pack's environmental benefits compared with similar products that use card instead of pulp, it would be churlish to criticize such a well thought-out product.

A recent study in the United States suggested that consumers prefer to buy sticking plasters in a plastic rather than a card pack; (inexplicably) they believe plastic is more environmentally friendly than card, because it can be recycled. The Help Remedies pulp packs seem to bridge that gap as they have some of the durability of plastic combined with the sustainability of card.

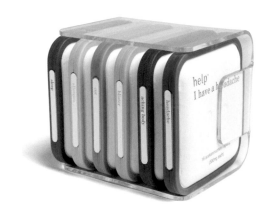

Help Remedies, designed by Chapps Malina

ECOLEAN

In the search for environmentally friendly liquid packaging formats, minimal weight combined with low cost and good performance is an ambitious goal. Plastic, even glass, bottles can go a long way to achieving these qualities, but there are limits to the amount of material that can be removed before they lose their structural integrity. Bags are lighter, but are usually less manageable for the same reason. Doy bags (free-standing pouches) in particular have been a major advance, but they tend to be restricted to single-serving applications, such as soups or detergent refills. More basic bag formats, where stability is less of an issue, need to be used as an element in a dispensing system, such as bags of milk used in conjunction with a plastic jug.

Ecolean, a Swedish-designed stand-up pouch, successfully addresses the imbalance between functionality and weight, by using calcium carbonate (chalk) as a bulking and stiffening agent in a multilayer PE format. The chalk element (which makes up 40 per cent of the pack) and the air-filled handle make the package significantly more rigid. The handle, combined with an easy-open spout, also makes the pack easy to use, even when it is half full, and as the bag is collapsible it allows viscous products, such as drinking yogurt, to be dispensed with little residue.

Although the pouch is multilayered with limited recycling potential its clear environmental advantage is its comparative weight. It weighs approximately half an equivalent volume gable-top carton. Ecolean's figures show that their pouches use significantly less energy and create less production waste than all the current standard paperboard and PET alternatives.

The bags are produced on a proprietary filling line using aseptically sealed envelopes from a continuously fed roll. These are slit open and filled with liquid, and the handles are inflated with compressed air, then the envelopes are sealed and shipped in outer cartons or pallets. Like gable-top packaging this system is extremely space-efficient before the bag is filled; unlike gable tops and PET bottles, the pouch compresses to its original shape after use so takes up much less space in the bin.

From a display perspective Ecolean stand-up pouches are fully printable, and their jug shape engagingly reflects their function. On the minus side they are not resealable. This may be acceptable, even environmentally preferable, for smaller sizes, but it forces consumers to improvise with some sort of peg or clip, which potentially limits the pack's applications. On the other hand, supplying a reusable clip might well be seen as an opportunity to underline Ecolean's environmental approach.

Despite several distinct environmental benefits consumer perception will eventually focus on Ecolean's lack of recyclability in comparison to gable-top packaging, so the pouch may face a challenging journey, but with company growth at 50 per cent per annum the trend is promising.

NOBOTTLE

The popularity of bottled water cannot be denied. It is convenient, beneficial to health and many people believe it tastes better than tap water. Whether out and about, at home or at work, they like to have a bottle of water handy, but consumers are becoming conscious of the huge amounts of fossil plastics it takes to quench this thirst for bottled water.

Since the late 1970s and early 1980s, when plastic bottles started to become a workable alternative to glass, manufacturers have been incrementally reducing their wall thickness, and today they are markedly lighter than their early counterparts. Nevertheless, disposable plastic bottles make a significant contribution to both landfill waste and the reprocessing output from recycled materials.

Sidel, a French manufacturer of packaging machinery, have made a huge leap forward in lightweighting with the introduction of NoBottle, and taken material reduction to its limits. They have eschewed the conventional thinking that a bottle needs to be a rigid structure. Instead, they have created one that is so thin most of its surface is more like a flexible membrane than a wall. In doing so they have managed to engineer a rigid base and comfortable waisted hand grip, blending lightness and practicality. This, combined with a strikingly attractive water droplet profile, makes the bottle a textbook example of form following function. The elastic membrane allows the water to become a part of the bottle structure, creating a distinctive jelly-like flexing effect that is not normally associated with PET, which is usually thought of as a relatively brittle form of plastic.

The standard 500-millilitre water bottle weighs approximately 16 grams, but Sidel have achieved a 40 per cent weight saving with their 9.9-gram NoBottle. Sidel claim that if every one of the 26.5 billion water bottles produced in 2007 had been a NoBottle it would translate into annual plastic savings of 160,000 tonnes worldwide.

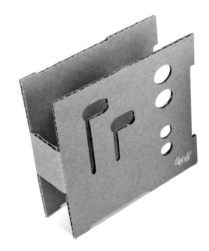

SENNHEISER CX-300 HEADPHONES

Packaging for small electronic goods tends to fall into three categories. Often it is purely functional, for transit, as high-value goods are usually either locked away in-store to prevent shoplifting or sent by post, which means the pack has little to do with merchandising the product.

Alternatively, when a product is displayed in-store it can be grotesquely overpackaged with layer upon layer of card and oversized vacuum formings. The relative merits of electronic goods on-shelf can be hard to compare when products are locked away in their pilfer-proof packaging, so excessive materials are used primarily to add value by increasing their shelf shout, although discouraging shoplifting may play a part.

The third type of pack falls between the two previous categories, as it is both functional and attractive. The focus is almost exclusively on the OOBE (out of box experience), which is a way of enhancing brand values even if a product is mailed or never seen until it is purchased.

Clearly this approach is potentially environmentally superior to the extravagant display packaging aimed at the impulse buyer, but OOBE-focused packs can also be excessive. Components are often laid out in space-consuming logical order to help the customer get the product up and running, or have unnecessary compartments and complex opening features.

Sennheiser's CX-300 headphone packaging shows how it should be done. Making use almost entirely of recycled corrugated card without glue, it challenges perceptions of how to do quality. Not only is it more environmentally friendly than conventional electronics goods packaging, but it works as both basic transit and OOBE packaging, and even looks engaging as a hanging pack despite the lack of product visibility.

The pack is simple, honest and devastatingly cool. It shows what can be achieved by relying on self-belief rather than simply ticking boxes.

Sennheiser headphones packaging

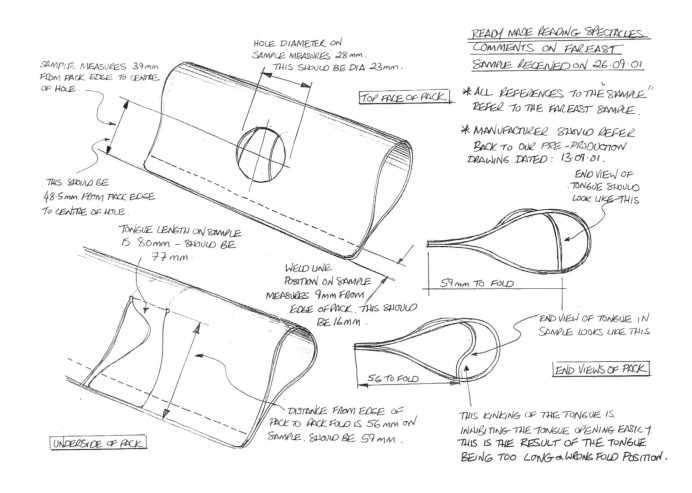

SAMPLE MEASURES 39mm FROM PACK EDGE TO CENTRE OF HOLE.

HOLE DIAMETER ON SAMPLE MEASURES 28 mm. THIS SHOULD BE DIA 23mm.

TOP FACE OF PACK

THIS SHOULD BE 48·5mm FROM PACK EDGE TO CENTRE OF HOLE.

TONGUE LENGTH ON SAMPLE IS 80mm - SHOULD BE 77mm.

WELD LINE POSITION ON SAMPLE MEASURES 9mm FROM EDGE OF PACK. THIS SHOULD BE 16mm.

DISTANCE FROM EDGE OF PACK TO PACK FOLD IS 56 mm ON SAMPLE. SHOULD BE 59 mm.

UNDERSIDE OF PACK

READY MADE READING SPECTACLES COMMENTS ON FAREAST SAMPLE RECEIVED ON 26·09·01

* ALL REFERENCES TO THE "SAMPLE" REFER TO THE FAREAST SAMPLE.

* MANUFACTURER SHOULD REFER BACK TO OUR PRE-PRODUCTION DRAWING DATED: 13·09·01.

END VIEW OF TONGUE SHOULD LOOK LIKE THIS

59 mm TO FOLD

END VIEW OF TONGUE IN SAMPLE LOOKS LIKE THIS

56 TO FOLD

END VIEWS OF PACK

THIS KINKING OF THE TONGUE IS INHIBITING THE TONGUE OPENING EASILY. THIS IS THE RESULT OF THE TONGUE BEING TOO LONG & WRONG FOLD POSITION.

BOOTS READY MADE READING GLASSES

The difficulty with creating packaging that can be reused is that unless it prevents another purchase, or reduces materials or saves energy, it has no particular environmental benefit. For instance, a bottle that can be reused as a toy may be fun and engaging, but will eventually be thrown away.

In 2002, Boots readymade reading glasses were sold as a premium product, but their crinkled polythene HDPE bag and cardboard hanging tag made them look distinctly ordinary. In addition, the existing design did not communicate adequately: reading glasses need to display ample clear information so that customers can distinguish between styles and lens strength (diopter).

The problem was how to make the packaging more premium and communicative while keeping it minimal.

There was clearly an opportunity to make it more customer-friendly, but this had to be done without adding significant cost or increasing the materials excessively.

The solution was to create a distinctive case for the glasses: a single piece of polypropylene (PP), welded along one edge, with a simple push-release integral locking tab to keep the glasses in place. A bold, coloured stripe shows the strength of magnification and is a strong, graphic feature that makes it easy for customers to quickly identify the lenses they need, even with impaired vision.

In effect, the design both added customer benefit and made an environmental contribution, as there is no need to buy an additional case for the glasses. It was also economical with materials, adding no more than 5 per cent to the overall packaging costs.

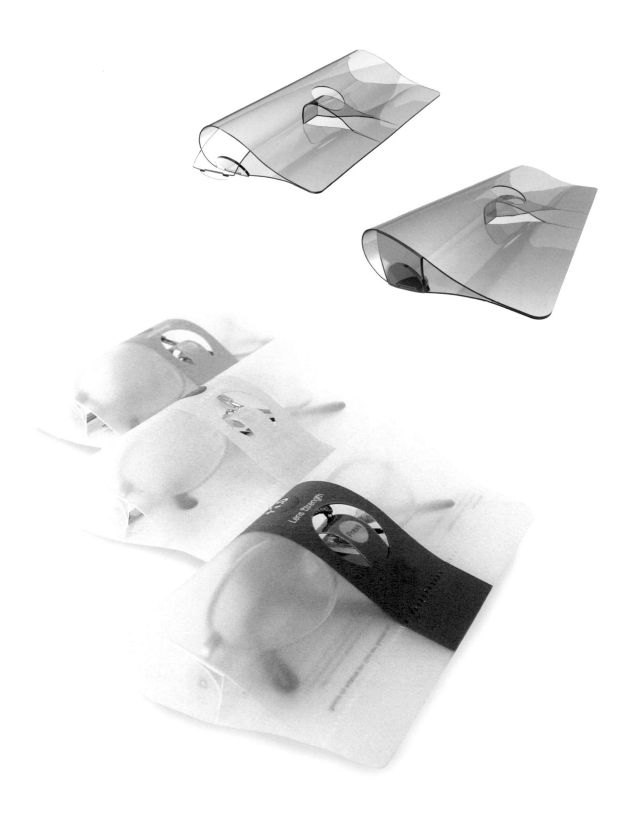

Boots ready made reading glasses

DIRECTORY
OF MATERIALS

PLASTICS

PLASTICS (POLYMERS) ARE A BY-PRODUCT OF OIL PRODUCTION, SO DO NOT ADD TO THE AMOUNT OF OIL EXTRACTED. MANY IN THE PACKAGING INDUSTRY WOULD ARGUE THAT THE PRODUCTION OF PLASTICS SHOULD BE SEEN NOT AS THE EXPLOITATION OF A FINITE RESOURCE, BUT RATHER THE EFFICIENT USE OF ONE THAT IS ALREADY EXPLOITED.

INTRODUCTION

- In total, plastic packaging uses only around 2 per cent of all crude oil produced.
- Despite being carbon-based, plastics break down extremely slowly, over hundreds of years, particularly in the oxygen-starved conditions of landfill. However, recent research has shown that with selective breeding it is possible to develop strains of bacteria that are capable of digesting plastics within a matter of weeks.
- Most of the plastics ever produced still exist in some kind of form.

Plastics in general have a great deal to offer in terms of shape, lightness and performance, but their environmental qualities vary according to whether or not they can be recycled, so depend largely on national recycling facilities.

In terms of shape, plastic bottles are far less restrictive than glass, and make a positive contribution to the environment through their lightness and recycling potential. Clear plastic bottles have the most potential for reusability; as regional reprocessing plants focus on clear PET and HDPE they are more likely than coloured ones to be efficiently recycled.

PET recycling symbol

PET plastics in production

PET *(POLYETHYLENE TEREPHTHALATE)*

+ clear / recylable / light / durable / low gas permeability / weldable

! high cost (compared to PVC) / average moulding detail when blow-moulded / brittle

Typically used to manufacture

- **clear bottles** *(see p. 207)* for soft drinks and concentrates, toiletries and detergents
- **thermoformed or injection-moulded trays** *(see p. 217)*
- **vacuum-formed dessert and yogurt pots** *(see pp. 213–14)*
- **blister and clam packs** *(see pp. 219–20)*
- **films** *(see p. 226)*
- **cartons** *(see p. 209)*; from sheet
- **pouches** (doy bags)/sachets *(see p. 212)*
- **jars** *(see p. 207)*
- **resealable tubs** *(see p. 214)*
- **clear presentation tubes** *(see p. 224)*
- **flow-wrap bags** *(see p. 225)*

Characteristics for packaging

PET, often loosely referred to as polyester as it is a member of the polyester family, is a (usually) crystal clear and slightly brittle polymer.

When blown it is not particularly good for picking up surface decoration, so moulding embellishments tend to be restricted to rib or grid patterns. PET is generally not used

for particularly complex shapes such as packs with handles, because it does not flow as well as PVC or HDPE. Large PET bottles sometimes have an additional polypropylene handle moulding either let into the side or attached below the neck.

Other variants include:

APET *(amorphous polyethylene terephthalate)*
A vacuum-formable version of PET.

PETG *(polyethylene terephthalate glycol)*
A more flexible form of PET with higher impact strength, used for vacuum forming. It takes print well, but is more expensive than regular APET.

Both APET and PETG are available in sheet form.

FPET
A film-grade PET, which can be used for lids and printed shrink-sleeving.

In many ways PET resembles PVC and has taken over many of its packaging roles, since the emissions caused by PVC and the additives it contains have an adverse effect on the environment. It is the plastic of choice for moulding clear bottles and is increasingly replacing PVC for clear vacuum formings.

PEN *(polyethylene napthalate)*
PEN is a realted polyester with better barrier properties than PET, so is more suited to applications such as beer bottles.

Manufacture

Bottles are usually injection blow-moulded or injection stretch-moulded by heating a pre-injection moulded preform (resembling a test tube), which is then blown into shape. PET bottles usually have a clear 'gate' dimple at the base where the plastic was injected to form the preform.

Larger carbonated-drinks bottles have dimpled feet at the base, which help contain the stresses caused by the additional pressure.

Reuse

PET bottles are collected for reuse in some European countries. A deposit or tax is paid to help fund the scheme.

Some PET bottles (for example, for hand soaps) are refillable, but there is plenty of scope to make this a more common practice.

Recycling

PET can easily be recycled, mainly because it is usually collected in the form of bottles and is normally clear, so colour variation in mixed recyclate is not an issue. It can be converted into rPET (recycled PET) and reused for bottles, cartons, punnets, clear thermoformed tubs and food trays, or polyester fibre. Blue and green PET may be collected for recycling, but other colour variants are unlikely to be converted into rPET.

Advances in reprocessing technology, through the more widespread introduction of plastics recovery facilities (PRFs) will allow a greater range of PET variants to be collected and will improve colour sorting.

After-use of PET – a fleece

Polyester fibre is much easier to produce than food-grade packaging, as contamination is less of an issue. It is typically used to manufacture clothing, such as fleeces or cheaper carpets.

Potential uses for recycled PET

PET bottles can be reprocessed into food-grade packaging, which is in considerable demand.

Other uses include fibre, tote bags, rPET bottles, fleece for clothing, training shoes, luggage, upholstery, furniture, carpets, fibrefill, industrial strapping, sheet and film, and automotive parts, including luggage racks, fuse boxes, bumpers, grilles and door panels.

Lightweighting

Although PET is brittle, it provides excellent opportunities for lightweighting. The example of Sidel's NoBottle and Krone's Nitropouch demonstrate the potential for blow-moulded PET bottles.

Biodegradability

PET is effectively non-biodegradable as it takes hundreds of years to break down.

Compostability

PET is non-compostable.

Incineration

PET combusts completely when it is incinerated, creating only water and carbon dioxide, so it is one of the least damaging plastics from an environmental point of view.

Landfill

In the anaerobic conditions of landfill PET is protected from bacterial action, so will take hundreds of years to degrade. This is not necessarily bad because it is effectively inert in comparison to plant-based materials that produce methane.

Moulding HDPE bottles

HDPE recycling symbol

HDPE (HIGH-DENSITY POLYETHYLENE)

➕ **low cost / recylable / durable / wide variety of surface effects / good moulding detail / lightweight compared to glass**

❗ **clear HDPE is slightly cloudy / coloured HDPE is unlikely to be recycled back into packaging / transporting empty bottles to the filling site is effectively shipping air, so on-site moulding is preferable / concerns over the unchecked proliferation of HDPE carrier bags**

Typically used to manufacture

- **opaque or translucent bottles** *(see p. 207)* for milk, toiletries, automotive lubricants, detergents, sauces, etc.
- **tottles** for cosmetics, sauces, etc. *(see p. 230 [pumps/atomizers])*
- **flip-top/screw-top closures** *(see p. 230)*
- **flow-wrap bags** *(see p. 225)*
- **carrier bags** *(see pp. 225-26)*
- **films** *(see p. 226)*
- **flexible tubes** for toiletries and creams *(see p. 224)*
- **jars** *(see p. 207)*

Characteristics for packaging

HDPE is much softer and more flexible than PET. It is translucent in its virgin state, but is often mixed with colours and additives to make attractive effects.

Moulded HDPE is good for surface detail, and is often pearlized or metallized and matched to the container lid (usually made from polypropylene). Handles are a common feature of larger bottles.

HDPE flows better than PET, but HDPE bottles need thicker walls, so would be heavier than an equivalent volume PET bottle. HDPE does not have the structural rigidity to contain carbonated drinks and is more gas permeable than PET.

HDPE is often used for carrier bags, as it has excellent tensile strength at low gauges which allows the minimal amount of material to be used.

Disposable HDPE carrier bags are seen as being a particularly wasteful use of plastic and are perhaps disproportionately blamed for harming marine life. In truth, all sorts of plastic waste contribute to the problem. This is highlighted by the great Pacific garbage patch, an area of floating waste perhaps as large as Texas, which is created by the eddying ocean currents of the North Pacific gyre.

Some governments, such as those of Ireland, Belgium and Hong Kong, are making increased efforts to encourage the reuse of carrier bags through retailer incentives or targeted taxation. Others, like those of Italy, Bangladesh, South Africa and Thailand, ban single-use bags completely.

Manufacture

HDPE bottles can be both injection blow-moulded or (more likely) extrusion blow-moulded. In the latter process an HDPE tube (parison) is effectively trapped at both ends by the mould and then blown into shape. This leaves a line detail across the top, which is hidden by the lid, and across the base.

Reuse

HDPE bottles are durable enough to be reused around the home, a quality that is underexploited by designers. There is also plenty of scope for them to be refilled, particularly in the case of more premium products, such as toiletries. However, as a formal environmental strategy the emphasis is strongly on recycling.

Recycling

While HDPE is recyclable, in practical terms only translucent containers are likely to be reprocessed into packaging, although it can be converted into garden furniture or mixed with wood waste and converted into wood-plastic composite (WPC), which is suitable for applications such as decking. This may be a short-term solution, as WPCs are non-recyclable and ultimately are likely to be incinerated or disposed of in landfill. As more efficient sorting methods are introduced at plastics recovery facilities and markets are established the picture will change.

HDPE film is also recycled, but it can be difficult to sort it from other plastic and degradable films. Often it is not collected for recycling because it is not always considered environmentally efficient to collect such a lightweight yet bulky material.

Carrier bag production

Potential uses for recycled HDPE

Non-carbonated bottles, building products, benches, recycling containers, picnic tables, fencing, synthetic lumber and bin liners.

Lightweighting

There are opportunities for lightweighting HDPE (which is already a lightweight material). Milk bottles, in particular, make good use of shape to combine durability with minimal material use

Biodegradability

HDPE is effectively non-biodegradable as it takes hundreds of years to break down.

Compostability

HDPE is non-compostable.

Incineration

HDPE combusts completely when incinerated, creating only water and carbon dioxide, but common additives, such as UV stabilizers, can create waste products.

Landfill

In the anaerobic conditions of landfill HDPE is protected from bacterial action, so it will take hundreds of years to degrade. This is not necessarily bad because it is effectively inert in comparison to plant-based materials that produce methane.

HDPE bottle reused as a paint-brush cleaning pot

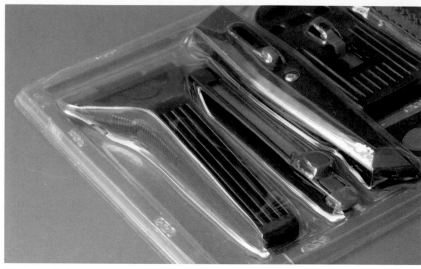

PVC recycling symbol

PVC blister packaging

PVC (POLYVINYL CHLORIDE)

➕ low cost / high clarity / durable / wide variety of surface effects / good moulding detail / weldable

❗ environmental doubts over processing emissions / evidence of links to cancer and infertility / can compromise PET recycling / transporting empty bottles to the filling site is effectively shipping air, so on-site moulding is preferable

Typically used to manufacture

- **clear and high-gloss coloured bottles** *(see p. 207)*, mostly non-food and particularly for automotive and hardware products, but also for some toiletries and concentrated juice drinks
- **blister and clam packs** *(see pp. 219–20)*
- **films** *(see p. 226)*, particularly for shrink-sleeving and for shrink-wrapping meat trays
- **flexible wallets** *(see p. 227)*
- **cartons** *(see p. 209)*
- **flexible tubes** for toiletries and creams *(see p. 224)*
- **blow-moulded jars** *(see p. 207)*
- **clear presentation tubes** *(see p. 224)*

Characteristics for packaging

PVC is arguably the most adaptable of all the plastics and, although it is still much used in manufacturing, particularly in the building trade, it was one of the first to cause environmental concerns. These relate to early studies that suggested dioxins were released during the manufacturing process and during incineration of PVC waste.

Vinyl chloride emissions and dioxins are linked to long-term health conditions, such as infertility and cancer, and, although the industry has dramatically improved manufacturing procedures, many environmental doubts persist – not least about some of the plasticizers used to make PVC softer, which have been shown to release toxic gases.

Moulded PVC is generally used on non-food packaging, particularly automotive and hardware products, but is still sometimes used for toiletries. For many applications, particularly clear bottles, it has been replaced directly by PET, but it remains popular for blister and clam packs because of its low cost and flexibility in comparison with PET.

PVC film, which has good oxygen permeability, is still used to wrap food trays, particularly ones for meat, as it allows the food to retain its colour for longer. Mainly as a result of the health concerns about PVC, LDPE has replaced PVC film for many of its common uses.

Manufacture

Inexpensive and extremely malleable, PVC gives moulded bottles the flexibility of HDPE and the clarity and shine of PET. Bottles are normally extrusion blow-moulded, so have a line detail across the base and neck.

Reuse

The options for reusing PVC tend to be limited, but there is no reason why PVC toiletry bottles, for instance, should not be refillable.

Recycling

PVC bottles can often be put out for kerbside collection, but vacuum formings are frequently not collected. Advances in technology are beginning to change the efficiency of PVC recovery.

Clear PVC bottles are a threat to the recycling of PET, because, like PLA, it has the potential to contaminate the recycling stream. PET reprocessors may reject an entire bale of plastic bottles if a single PVC one is found. For this reason, PVC shrink sleeves should not be applied to PET bottles.

A great deal of PVC is exported for reprocessing in developing economies. There are doubts whether proper precautions are taken to protect workers from harmful emissions during the process.

Potential uses for recycled PVC

Binders, decking, car parts, guttering, flooring, cable sheathing, speed humps.

Lightweighting

PVC vacuum formings could be said to be a lightweight alternative to other types of packaging. In its flexible form PVC wallets and bags can be a lighter and more attractive alternative to card, but these small environmental benefits are massively outweighed by the environmental damage caused by PVC's production and eventual disposal.

Reusable PVC crayon packaging

Biodegradability

PVC is effectively non-biodegradable. It takes hundreds of years to break down and releases toxins in the process.

Compostability

PVC is non-compostable.

Incineration

PVC emits chlorine, hydrogen chloride and dioxins when incinerated, but the extent to which they damage the environment depends on the efficiency of the incinerator.

Landfill

There are concerns about the long-term effects of PVC in landfill because of the potential damaging effects of chemical additives leaching into the soil and water table.

LDPE recycling symbol

LDPE reusable carrier bag

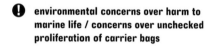

LDPE (LOW-DENSITY POLYETHYLENE)

➕ **low cost / lightweight / flexible / moisture-resistant / weldable**

❗ **environmental concerns over harm to marine life / concerns over unchecked proliferation of carrier bags**

Typically used to manufacture

- **flow-wrap bags** *(see p. 225)*
- **carrier bags** *(see pp. 225–26)*
- **bottles** *(see p. 207)*; for example, flexible laboratory bottles
- **lids** *(see p. 230)*; for example, milk bottle lids
- **six-pack holders** *(see p. 222)*
- **films** *(see p. 226)*
- **flexible tubes** *(see p. 224)*; for example, for toiletries, sauces
- **transit packaging**; polyethylene foam *(see pp. 231–32)*
- **jars** *(see p. 206)*
- **trays/punnets** *(see p. 216)*
- **pouches** (doy bags)/sachets *(see p. 212)*
- **beverage cartons** *(see p. 210)*
- **dessert pots** *(see p. 214)*

Characteristics for packaging

LDPE is usually seen in the form of freezer and carrier bags – HDPE is more commonly used for the latter, but heavyweight reusable versions are usually made from LDPE. It is also laminated to other materials, such as paperboard, to provide barrier properties or allow them to be heat-sealed.

LLDPE (linear polyethylene) is more malleable than LDPE with a higher tensile strength and has replaced many of its uses, such as for stretch films.

When moulded, LDPE is softer and more flexible than HDPE.

Manufacture

LDPE is an inexpensive soft material. It is usually extruded as a film, but may be moulded for bottle caps or blow-moulded as bottles.

Reuse

LDPE carrier bags have almost become the standard-bearer for reusability. Retailers have made great strides in reducing their consumption and in the United Kingdom one of the ways they have achieved this has been by offering sturdy 'bags for life' and making a small charge for standard carrier bags.

Recycling

Although bags are widely collected, LDPE bag recycling has become less straightforward as a result of the widespread use of biodegradable carrier bags, which can compromise the resulting recyclate.

Moulded LDPE is not usually retrieved from post-consumer waste, for recycling.

Potential uses for recycled LDPE

Film and sheet, bin liners, compost bins, waste bins, lumber.

Lightweighting

Bags are the ultimate in lightweight packaging, but LDPE can be laminated to other lightweight materials, such as paperboard, to make them waterproof. This is commonly seen in beverage cartons and premium dessert pots.

Biodegradability

LDPE breaks down over hundreds of years. However, additives can be used to make it degradable, effectively by causing it to break down into very small pieces.

Compostability

LDPE is non-compostable.

Incineration

LDPE combusts completely when incinerated, creating only water and carbon dioxide, but common additives can create waste products.

Landfill

In the anaerobic conditions of landfill LDPE is protected from bacterial action, so will take hundreds of years to degrade. This is not necessarily bad because it is effectively inert in comparison to plant-based materials that produce methane.

PP recycling symbol

PP moulded components

PP *(POLYPROPYLENE)*

 robust / rigid / resistant to high temperatures / detailed moulding / excellent surface detail

 often not recyclable (although this varies by country)

Typically used to manufacture

- **resealable tubs** *(see p. 214)*
- **flip-top/screw-top closures** *(see p. 230)*
- **pull-tops** *(see p. 230)*
- **injection-moulded trays/punnets** *(see p. 217)*
- **films** *(see p. 226)*
- **bottles** *(see p. 207)*
- **cartons** *(see p. 209)*; folded from sheet
- **flexible tubes** *(see p. 224)* for toiletries and creams
- **flow-wrap bags** *(see p. 225)*
- **carrier bags** *(see pp. 225–26)*
- **jars** *(see p. 207)*
- **pumps** *(see p. 230)*
- **trigger tops** *(see p. 230)*
- **pouches (doy bags)/sachets** *(see p. 212)*
- **transit packaging** *(see pp. 231–32)*

Characteristics for packaging

In its 'natural' state PP is slightly cloudy, but not as opaque as HDPE. It is often coloured. It usually takes the form of plastic tubs or caps, but is sometimes used for roll-on deodorants or bottles with a high degree of surface detailing. It is also used in sheet form to make cartons and hangers. Film variants of PP include:

OPP (oriented polypropylene)

BOPP (biaxially oriented polypropylene)

Manufacture

PP is usually injection-moulded, but may be blow-moulded, cast in sheet form or extruded as a film.

Reuse

PP multitrip transit crates are used in retailing for distribution, and have widely replaced single-use corrugated cartons.

Reuse in the home tends to be informal. For example, PP ice-cream tubs or resealable soup pots make excellent reusable freezer containers.

Robust PP folded gift cartons are often marketed with the potential of reusability, but it is doubtful whether many of the instances of reuse make any particular environmental contribution.

Recycling

PP has good potential for recycling but is not universally collected. Advances in recovery techniques will improve its recycling rates.

Potential uses for recycled PP

Car parts, gardening products, buckets, bins.

Lightweighting

There may be some scope for lightweighting PP, particularly for resealable pots and tubs that sometimes seem to use an excessive amount of material.

Biodegradability

PP is effectively non-biodegradable as it breaks down over hundreds of years.

Compostability

PP is non-compostable.

Incineration

PP combusts completely when incinerated, creating only water and carbon dioxide, but common additives can create waste products.

Landfill

In the anaerobic conditions of landfill PP is protected from bacterial action, so will take hundreds of years to degrade. This is not necessarily bad, because it is relatively inert in comparison to plant-based materials that produce methane.

PS recycling symbol

PS food tray

PS *(POLYSTYRENE)*

 insulating / impact absorbent (as foam) flexible

 brittle / can be inefficient to recycle (particularly in foam form)

Typically used to manufacture

- **pots** *(see pp. 213–14)*
- **trays** for fruit, vegetables and meat; foam *(see pp. 216–17)*
- **burger boxes**; foam *(see p. 222)*
- **transit packaging**; polystyrene foam chips *(see pp. 231–32)*
- **injection-moulded jars** *(see p. 207)* for cosmetics

Characteristics for packaging

PS (styrene) is clear and colourless in its 'natural' state. In packaging it normally takes two very different forms: the hard, brittle white plastic used to form yogurt pots and dairy spread tubs; and, in its foamed version, meat trays and burger boxes. Despite being lightweight and shock absorbent, it has largely been replaced for transit packaging by moulded pulp and air-filled film envelopes that are more easily recycled and compressed, although it is still frequently used for heat-insulated transport packaging. PS is extremely flexible when heated, which makes it ideal for thermoforming, but it is often also seen as clear injection-moulded cosmetics packaging.

Manufacture

PS can be injection-moulded, thermoformed or foamed.

Reuse

There are few opportunities to reuse PS as it is brittle in its rigid form and easily dented as a foam. Loose-fill polystyrene foam chips in transit packaging are perhaps the only obvious example of effective reuse.

Recycling

Although PS is recyclable, post-consumer waste styrene is by and large not widely recycled. Advances in recovery techniques will improve its recycling.

Potential uses for recycled PS

Thermal insulation, panelling, egg cartons, foam packing, takeaway food containers.

Lightweighting

PS is ideal for lightweight applications.

Biodegradability

PS is effectively non-biodegradable because it breaks down over hundreds of years, but advances in bacteriology show potential for speeding up the process dramatically.

Non-biodegradability is perhaps a more acute problem with the foamed form of PS than it is with many other plastics, as the foam is easily is blown around in wind. This not only creates a high-profile litter problem, but, more seriously, the foam can easily get into waterways where it eventually becomes a hazard to marine life. However, foamed PS quickly degrades into smaller and smaller pieces which mitigates its damage to some extent.

Compostability

PS is non-compostable, but there are biodegradable alternatives to foamed PS, such as foamed starch.

Incineration

PS combusts completely when it is incinerated at high temperatures, and produces mainly water and carbon dioxide.

Landfill

In the anaerobic conditions of landfill PS is protected from bacterial action, so will take hundreds of years to degrade.

GLASS

ADVANCES IN LIGHTWEIGHTING HAVE MADE GLASS MUCH MORE ATTRACTIVE AS AN ENVIRONMENTALLY FRIENDLY MATERIAL, WITH GREAT POTENTIAL FOR DESIGNERS. DESPITE ITS COMPARATIVE WEIGHT AND HIGH ENERGY CONSUMPTION, IT ALSO HAS SIGNIFICANT BARRIER PROPERTIES THAT SET IT APART FROM PLASTIC. GLASS IS WIDELY COLLECTED AND EASILY RECYCLED OR, WITH THE RIGHT COLLECTION INFRASTRUCTURE, REUSED. SEVERAL COUNTRIES HAVE BOTTLE-DEPOSIT TAXATION SYSTEMS, WHICH DRAMATICALLY IMPROVE RECOVERY RATES. PUBLIC PERCEPTION OF GLASS IS GENERALLY POSITIVE DESPITE ITS RELATIVELY POOR ENVIRONMENTAL PROFILE.

Glass is reused as aggreagate in road surfaces

INTRODUCTION

+ infinitely recyclable / durable / reusable / better barrier material than plastics / can have recycled content / inert

! high cost compared with other container materials / high use of energy in production and recycling / high weight compared with plastic, which means transporting glass uses more energy / glass containers have to be empty when they are transported to the bottling plant

Typically used to manufacture

- **bottles** *(see p. 206)* for alcoholic beverages, concentrated soft drinks, sauces, fragrances
- **jars** *(see p. 206)* for preserves, sauces, cosmetics

Characteristics for packaging

Glass is a high-quality, durable traditional material, which is often used to convey an impression of quality and luxury. It has excellent gas-barrier properties, which make it the material of choice for most alcoholic beverages, but has been supplanted by PET, a cheaper, lighter (and arguably much more eco-friendly) alternative for soft drinks.

Manufacture

Glass is manufactured by heating silica (quartz sand) with sodium ash and lime (calcium oxide) at temperatures of around 1500˚C (2732˚F). The process is hugely energy-intensive and furnaces cannot be allowed to cool, so glassmaking is a 24-hour process.

Recycled glass (or cullet) is an important element in creating new glass: it is usually put in the furnace with the raw materials to help reduce processing temperatures.

Reuse

Glass is well suited to reuse because of its durability – some bottles can be reused up to 30 times. Doorstep milk deliveries are an example of a successful reuse system, where delivery, collection and refilling are handled, usually locally, by one company.

Some countries and states operate a bottle-deposit tax system, which encourages high return rates and allows glass bottles of a generic design to be reused many times over by different manufacturers or be recycled. Costly commercial deposit schemes have suffered as a result of competition from single-use PET.

Recycling

Glass was the first material to be widely recycled, and continues to be one of the most recycled with widespread local facilities at supermarkets, municipal waste sites and street corners. The current demand is such that the recyclate is often at a premium. Glass can be recycled ad infinitum without any deterioration in quality, but clear recycled glass tends to have a slight greenish tint because of contamination by coloured or tinted glass. In general, producing recycled glass uses significantly less energy than making virgin glass.

Glass used for packaging is predominantly flint (clear), amber or green. The maximum recycled content for glass is typically:

Recycled flint

60 per cent maximum cullet content

Recycled amber

65 per cent maximum cullet content

Recycled green

90 per cent maximum cullet content

In the United Kingdom and North America a disproportionate amount of green glass is collected for recycling, so, to prevent it being used as building aggregate or sent to Europe WRAP have practical suggestions for designers:

- Move to green-coloured containers wherever possible. For instance, if it is not necessary for the product to be visible the container could be sleeved or coated.
- Accept a lower clarity specification for flint, including a shade-of-green tint.
- Move from flint to amber, if the product colour permits.

This practical approach to designing with recycled glass can be used worldwide, and varied to suit local colour surpluses.

Recycled content varies from country to country. For instance, WRAP report that French wine bottles typically have 99 per cent recycled content and Bulgaria only 30 per cent, with a European average of 80.9 per cent.

Potential uses for recycled glass

Recycled glass has the same uses as virgin glass. There is no drop in quality, but there may be some variation in tint.

Lightweighting

Much of the current focus in designing with glass relates to lightweighting. Drinks manufacturers are often under government pressure to save energy by reducing material weight, and also benefit from reduced transport and handling costs.

For the designer it is important to work in collaboration with the glass manufacturer from an early stage, as the lightweighting process places some restrictions on the profiles available. In a nutshell, the softer the shape the better. Also, time must be allowed for trialling the design to ensure it is robust enough for transportation and retailing.

Biodegradability

Glass is non-biodegradable.

Compostability

Glass is non-compostable.

Incineration

Because glass is inert, with a high melting point, it remains in the bottom ash in the incinerator.

Landfill

Unlike other materials such as paper and plastics, glass does not deteriorate in landfill, emit greenhouse gases or leach toxins into the water table.

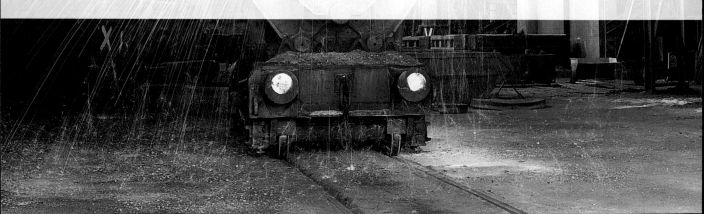

METALS

ALUMINIUM AND STEEL ARE IMPORTANT PACKAGING MATERIALS THAT ARE USED PARTICULARLY FOR THEIR BARRIER PROPERTIES AND STRENGTH.

METAL CONTAINERS CAN BE SHAPED TO SOME EXTENT AND IT IS NOT UNUSUAL TO SEE WAISTED AEROSOLS FOR FRAGRANCES, AND EVEN ALUMINIUM BEVERAGE BOTTLES. MAKING SCULPTURAL CHANGES TO THE CYLINDRICAL FORM OF AEROSOLS IS A GOOD WAY FOR LARGER COMPANIES TO GIVE A PRODUCT MORE PERSONALITY AND DIFFERENTIATE THEMSELVES FROM OWN-BRAND ME-TOO PRODUCTS.

BOTH ALUMINIUM AND STEEL ARE WIDELY RECYCLED.

Aluminium recycling symbol

Aluminium ingots

ALUMINIUM

➕ lightweight / cheap / easily and efficiently recycled / shapes can be customized / can have recycled content

❗ aluminium production uses a great deal of energy / cans are usually shipped empty to the beverage manufacturer

Typically used to manufacture

- **beverage cans** *(see p. 210)*
- **bottles** *(see p. 206)*
- **aerosols** *(see p. 208)*
- **trays** *(see p. 216)*
- **doy bags** (pouches)/sachets *(see p. 212)*
- **foils** *(see p. 215)*
- **screw-top closures** *(see p. 229)*
- **beverage cartons** *(see p. 210)*
- **flow-wrap bags** *(see p. 225)*
- **lids** *(see p. 229)* for foods, pharmaceuticals, cosmetics
- **spiral-wound tubes** *(see p. 223)* for dry foods
- **pie cases, containers** for takeaway foods *(see p. 215 [foils])*

Characteristics for packaging

Aluminium is made from alumina, which is extracted from bauxite, and is the world's most abundant metal. Producing the raw material takes a great deal of energy, but recycling it uses up to 95 per cent less. Because it is an efficient, lightweight barrier material it can be laminated to plastics or card as a foil.

The wall thickness of aluminium beverage cans is often less than a human hair, so they are an environmentally efficient form of packaging, although it might be argued that aluminium production in general is not green.

Aluminium aerosols and bottles can be sculpted to a certain extent to create custom profiles.

Manufacture

Production of aluminium is a two-stage process. First, alumina is extracted from bauxite by mixing it with caustic soda and heating it under pressure. It then goes through refining, filtration, precipitation and calcination processes to obtain uncontaminated raw alumina. In the second stage, the alumina is mixed with cryolite and electrically charged at an extremely high voltage to create molten aluminium.

Aluminium cans start their lives as discs (blanks) punched from aluminium sheet. These go through a series of operations during which they are forced through shaping rings in order to stretch their walls. Once the base and wall have been formed, any excess is trimmed and the cans are labelled by a 'decorator'. The interiors are then sprayed with a protective coating. The can-ends are pressed from blanks and a sealant is applied to the underside. Finally, the pull-tab is applied to the top surface of the can-end and both cans and ends are shipped to the beverage manufacturer for filling and sealing.

The impact-extrusion process for making aerosols and bottlecans is broadly similar, but the resultant wall thicknesses are at least three times those of beverage cans. Some manufacturers cite the improved insulation qualities as an advantage. Both bottlecans and aerosols go through a die-necking process to reduce the neck. Further swaging and shaping options are available to create a growing palette of profiles.

Trays are pressed from aluminium sheet.

Reuse

Because the material is durable there are opportunities for trays to be reused around the home, but aluminium packaging tends to be single-use.

Recycling

Aluminium is extremely efficient to recycle, which mitigates its energy-intensive primary production. Cans, aerosols and trays are widely collected for recycling, both from the kerbside and at recycling centres.

Thin-wall laminated pouches are an efficient, lightweight form of packaging, but it is not currently practical to recycle them.

Potential uses for recycled aluminium

Recycled aluminium cans and aerosols can be recycled into more cans and aerosols, and can be used in most sectors of industry to make aluminium products.

Foil trays have a softer alloy than aluminium cans, and are often reprocessed into items such as lightweight engine components.

Bauxite mining

Lightweighting

Aluminium lends itself to lightweighting and is often used as an alternative to heavier forms of packaging; for instance, foil pouches have excellent barrier qualities and often replace steel food cans. Beverage cans have progressively been lightweighted over decades.

Aluminium is also laminated to lightweight card to create aseptic beverage cartons.

Biodegradability

Aluminium is non-biodegradable.

Compostability

Aluminium is non-compostable.

Incineration

Aluminium melts when it is incinerated, and can be reclaimed from the bottom ash.

Landfill

Aluminium oxidizes to aluminium oxide and takes approximately 300 years to break down completely. There is some discussion about mining landfill for aluminium.

Steel recycling symbol

Steel cans being formed

STEEL

➕ **cheap / easily recycled**

❗ **steel production uses a great deal of energy / cans are usually shipped empty to the food or beverage manufacturer**

Typically used to manufacture

- **tins for storage/presentation** (see p. 212)
- **aerosols** (see p. 208)
- **beverage and food cans** (see p. 211)
- **crown caps, twist lids** (see p. 229)

Characteristics for packaging

Steel was one of the first packaging materials to be used for the mass production of preserved foods. The earliest cannery opened in 1813, and it was not until the arrival of frozen foods in the 1930s that steel had significant competition as a means of preserving food. As the century progressed its dominance was challenged by plastics and aluminium.

Steel is relatively abundant and inexpensive, and while its weight and lack of flexibility have created limitations to its use, it remains extremely popular for mass-produced packaging formats, such as food and beverage cans. It is still used for presentation tins, a format that allows more sculptural variety. In the past, steel has been used for a variety of shaped containers, such as Sapporo beer cans and Teisseire fruit syrup, but to a large extent aluminium has replaced it as a medium for creating custom profiles.

Teisseire shaped-steel juice bottle

Manufacture

Steel production is an extremely energy-intensive process, with high emissions and water consumption. It is an alloy of iron and carbon, and was first mass-produced from pig iron – made by heating iron ore, coke (from coal) and limestone in a blast furnace – using the Bessemer converter technique. Pig iron was crucial to the Industrial Revolution, but it is full of impurities that need to be removed to create steel, which is much stronger and more adaptable. The Bessemer converter was a huge clay lined tilting drum, which allowed a blast of air to flow through the molten pig iron, burning off excess carbon and other impurities. Molten steel was then poured out of the drum to be cast into ingots.

Today, several different processes are used to make steel. The Bessemer converter has been superseded by the much more efficient basic oxygen process (which uses oxygen instead of air) and the electric arc furnace which is typically used to recycle steel scrap.

Steel beverage cans are made in a similar way to aluminium ones. They start their lives as discs (blanks) punched from steel sheet. These go through a series of operations where they are forced through shaping rings to stretch their walls. Once the base and wall have been formed any excess is trimmed and the cans are labelled by a 'decorator'. The interiors of the cans are then sprayed with a protective coating. The can-end is pressed from a blank and a sealant is applied to the underside. Finally, the pull-tab is applied to the top surface of the can-end and both cans and ends are

shipped to the beverage manufacturer for filling and sealing.

To make food cans the bodies are formed from flat sheet steel fed from a coil. This is coated on the inside and decorated on the outside, if printing is required. Finally, it is welded into a cylinder and the ends are flanged in readiness to receive the end pieces.

The process for making aerosol cans is similar to that for food cans. Steel aerosols can usually be identified by a vertical seam and end caps at the top and base.

Steel containers such as biscuit tins, tea caddies and gift boxes have a vertical, seamed middle section with separate base and lid section, and a variety of edge details.

Reuse

With its strong presentational element and excellent durability, steel lends itself to reuse. Classically, the biscuit tin becomes a cake tin, but there are any number of steel-branded caddies, pots and containers that can last for generations. Which is excellent, but it is worth remembering all the others that end up in landfill. Heavy-duty tins are heavy users of energy and reuse cannot be relied on as an environmental strategy for steel.

Recycling

It is extremely easy to separate steel packaging from household waste with electromagnets, so the recovery rate is high: recycling uses around 75 per cent less than making steel from iron ore. The downside is that the price for recovered steel can be so low that, in commercial terms, it is often not worth collecting it.

Potential uses for recycled steel

Recycled steel is indistinguishable from the virgin material, so it can be used for anything from battleships to bollards.

Lightweighting

Great strides have been made in lightweighting steel containers, but more can be done. Beverage cans have walls as thin as a human hair, yet tinplate boxes have made little progress.

Biodegradability

Steel oxidizes (rusts) when left in the open, rather than strictly biodegrading.

Compostability

Steel is non-compostable.

Landfill

Steel does not break down quickly in landfill, and neither does it create harmful emissions. It is easily extracted from municipal solid waste with electromagnets, which greatly reduces the amount that reaches landfill.

Incineration

Steel is non-combustible and can be removed from incinerated waste with electromagnets.

PAPER AND CARD

PAPER HAS EXCEPTIONAL QUALITIES, WITH MANY POTENTIAL STRUCTURAL USES INCLUDING BAGS, ENVELOPES, LABELS AND WRAPS. CARD – IN MANY WAYS THE MOST HARD-WORKING PACKAGING MATERIAL – NOT ONLY HAS EXCELLENT STRUCTURAL AND SCULPTURAL QUALITIES, BUT IS ALSO AN EXCEPTIONAL MEDIUM FOR GRAPHICS. ALL TOO OFTEN, THOUGH, IT IS USED SIMPLY AS A GRAPHIC WRAP FOR HARD-TO-LABEL PACKS OR, WORSE, TO GIVE MULTIPACKS ADDITIONAL GRAPHIC PRESENCE.

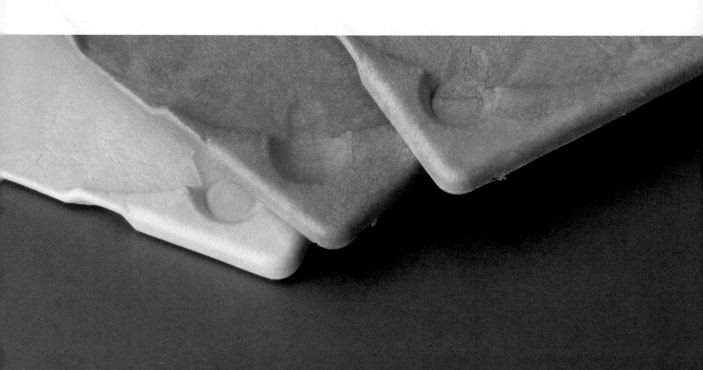

INTRODUCTION

Card is sustainable (from the right source), compostable, recyclable, versatile and inexpensive. The trouble with cardboard boxes is that they often look boring, despite card's sculptural potential, which tends to be underexploited. To some extent this is because complex card-folding is usually more time-consuming than popping up a preglued carton, and does not usually lend itself to high-speed machine assembly.

The latter is a massive advantage for a smaller company, as it enables them to use sculptural form to add value in a way that a much larger one with high-speed packaging lines would have difficulty replicating. Nevertheless, however complex a pack may be, it still has to work in a retail environment, so stacking and stability are essential qualities that must never be neglected. And, of course, even the dullest rectangular carton can be given presence with unusual proportions, a quirky window position or surprising embossing.

Although a great deal of forestry for the production of paper pulp leaves much to be desired, in general it does not involve taking land away from food production. In many areas (Europe in particular) more trees are being planted than felled.

PAPER

Typically used to manufacture

- **labels** *(see p. 228)*
- **wraps for pots** *(see p. 214 [pots])*
- **bags** *(see pp. 225–26)*
- **inserts** *(see p. 228)*
- **dessert pots** *(see p. 214)*
  resealable tubs *(see p. 214)*; polycard
  beverage cartons *(see p. 210)*;
  multilayer polycard

CARD/CARDBOARD

➕ **biodegradable / compostable / recyclable / sustainable / low cost**

❗ **high use of energy in production / production can be polluting / managed forests can be a threat to biodiversity / card can be heavy, particularly when recycled**

Typically used to manufacture

- **cartons** *(see p. 209)*
- **sleeves/envelopes** *(see p. 228)*
- **trays** *(see p. 217)*
- **swing tags** *(see p. 228)*
- **transit packaging** *(see pp. 231–32)*, structural supports
- **spiral-wound tubes** *(see p. 223)*
- **backboards** for blister packs *(see p. 220)*
- **backboards** for vacuum skin packaging *(see p. 223)*

Characteristics for packaging

Paper and card are usually derived from managed pine forests, but can come from a variety of fibrous sources, including bagasse (sugar-cane fibre), palm fibre, bamboo, hemp, flax, kenaf, wheat straw, reeds and rice straw.

While paper and card might be viewed as sustainable materials, some considerably unsustainable practices can be involved in their production. For example, there is a great deal of controversy about the process of paper production: paper mills are the fourth largest source of industrial pollution. They are blamed for 20 per cent of China's waterway pollution, and a paper mill was the first factory to be shut down under the country's new environmental pollution laws. The mills use large volumes of fresh water along with chlorine to bleach the paper, and kaolin for coatings as well as calcium carbonate, starch and titanium. The residues are often flushed away into rivers. Better-managed mills filter and recycle their water, using wood waste as an energy source.

The forestry process itself can also have a damaging effect on biodiversity, as mixed woodland or forest is typically replaced by a single species of the same age. Managing woodland as an industrial-scale farming process can have a dramatic effect on wildlife.

Accreditation schemes, such as the Forestry Stewardship Council, have a set of environmental standards to ensure timber is produced sustainably, with more care for the environment.

Manufacture

Wood can be either chemically or mechanically pulped. The chemical process produces the higher grade of pulp as it preserves the structural cellulose fibres better than mechanical pulping, washing away the lignin that binds the fibres together. However, it is not as efficient and produces less pulp, with a yield of around 50 per cent of the original wood.

Chemical pulping is used to produce kraft paper, which is used for brown paper bags

Various pulp packaging components

and brown corrugated cartons. The lignin is dissolved from the wood in a heated bath of water and chemicals, called a digester, then washed to create the basic pulp. At this stage it can be further processed to make white paper by 'bleaching', where it is typically treated with a mixture of chlorine and chlorine dioxide.

The mechanical process is harsher on the fibres: it steams then crushes the wood between two rollers and soaks it in water. It produces paper that is more brittle, prone to yellowing (because the lignin is not dissolved) and has a shorter life, but it is much more efficient than mechanical pulping as it converts most of the wood to paper.

In both cases the diluted pulp is poured on to a fast-moving mesh screen and pressed to remove excess liquid. The paper is then dried. Additives such as china clay and sizes can be applied to the pulp to improve the printing surface of the finished paper.

Reuse

There are limited opportunities for reusing cardboard cartons. It is not uncommon for them (and rigid envelopes) to be reused informally for mailing. This simple economy can be extended more formally to mail-order products when a new item replaces an older product that has to be returned. Instead of providing a special returns carton, as is often the case, it makes far more sense to design reusable packaging for the replacement product, so that this can be used to return the old item.

Recycling

Paper and card can be recycled up to eight times before the fibres become too short to provide any structure, and many mills are set up purely for this purpose, particularly in countries with limited forestry industries. Recycling them requires between 28 per cent and 70 per cent less energy than is needed to make them from raw materials.

Once the pulp has been de-inked and staples, bindings and glue have been removed, the production process is similar to that of virgin paper and involves bleaching and coating the finished paper (or card). However, some virgin pulp has to be added to maintain the paper's structural integrity. Mills produce a wide variety of papers and cards, in different ways.

Cardboard often has a 100 per cent recycled core, and facing layers with surfaces suitable for high-quality graphics. It may not only be heavier than a board of equivalent strength made from virgin pulp, but may also have poorer deadfold qualities.

It is possible to use 100 per cent recycled board or paper. Many variants are available, but clearly those that are the least bleached, processed and varnished, and that use biodegradable inks, are the most environmentally friendly and easiest to recycle or compost. Paper pulp with a high recycled content is not always suitable for packaging that comes into direct contact with food, as pulp sourced from mixed recycling can be contaminated by other materials.

Card and paper can easily be affected by food residue or broken glass in the increasingly popular co-mingled recycling collections, which makes them unsuitable for this type of recycling. And a recent study has found that toxic mineral oils from recycled newsprint in card can migrate through plastic films, so that food is contaminated. This may lead to tighter regulation of recycled content or limit the uses of recycled card.

Potential uses for recycled paper and card

Once paper and card have been repulped they can be used for many of the same applications as virgin paper and card.

Recycled paper pulp can be used to make moulded pulp products (see recycled paper pulp, p. 180), lower-grade boards, insulation or padding, and can be mixed with wood pulp to make partially recycled products.

Lightweighting

From an environmental point of view there are conflicting approaches to using carton board, one of the most common packaging materials, which is used for printed retail packaging of all sorts. While cardboard with a recycled core can perform in a similar way to standard carton board, it is heavier, so more energy-hungry in its transportation. Newer structural cardboards can have a lightweight core combined with rigid, high-quality graphic surfaces, which allows substantial weight savings to be made.

Lightweight board is popular with retailers because, to a large extent, they focus on reducing the weight of materials, rather than recycling.

Biodegradability

Because they are derived from fibre, paper and card are biodegradable.

Compostability

Paper and card are often compostable, both at home with garden waste or in an industrial composter, but some types of printing and laminated surfaces can make them unsuitable for composting. Some studies suggest that no more than 10 per cent of paper and card should be combined with plant material, so composting is only a partial answer to paper waste, and in most countries it is unlikely to be collected for composting with plant waste.

Incineration

Incineration and energy recovery is a better and more practical option than landfill for paper and card.

Landfill

Disposing of paper and card in landfill sites is not environmentally friendly, as they biodegrade anaerobically and emit methane.

MOULDED PULPS

MOULDED PULP PACKAGING IS MORE EXPENSIVE TO PRODUCE THAN CARD, BECAUSE OF ITS MOULDING COSTS, POOR PRINT FINISH AND THE RELATIVE INEFFICIENCY OF STACKING AND TRANSPORTING THE MOULDED SHAPES.

INTRODUCTION

It is underexploited, and tends to be used as transit packaging, or as a greener alternative to expanded polystyrene; its most high-profile use is as egg boxes. Recently, even such utilitarian products have undergone something of a makeover, demonstrating some of the potential of pulp packaging. Pulp is now being used for products with a more aesthetic environmental agenda, such as Help Remedies *(see p. 138)* and Method cleaning products *(see p. 122)*.

Pulp made from softwood is the most familiar type, but there are many other sources, each with slightly different characteristics. These include bagasse (sugar-cane fibre), palm fibre and bamboo; cotton, hemp, flax, kenaf, wheat straw, reeds and rice straw are also routinely pulped.

Like most plant-based materials pulps emit methane if landfilled, but can be recycled with paper-based products.

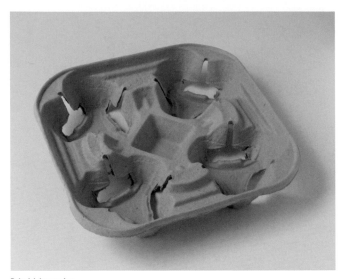

Pulp drinks carrier

RECYCLED PAPER PULP

➕ **recycled content / cheap / readily available / diverse uses**

❗ **the moulding process uses a large amount of energy and water, and reprocessing the recycled paper into pulp uses a great deal of energy, water and chemicals**

Typically used to manufacture

- **transit packaging** *(see pp. 231–32)*
- **egg boxes** *(see p. 222)*
- **trays** for fruit and vegetables *(see p. 217)*
- **burger boxes** *(see p. 222)*

Characteristics for packaging

Moulded paper pulp contains a high proportion of recycled paper, and virgin pulp may be added to make it stronger, as recycling shortens the cellulose fibres and reduces tensile strength. This high recycled content means it is not always suitable for packaging that comes in direct contact with food, as paper sourced from mixed recycling can be contaminated by other materials.

Manufacture

The pulp is typically moulded from slurry sprayed on to a drum that holds fine mesh moulds. It is sucked against the moulds and the mouldings are then dried. A finer finish and thinner walls can be achieved by using the double pressing (or hot pressing) method of manufacture where the pulp is squeezed into shape between two moulds.

Although moulded, recycled paper pulp provides products with excellent protection against impact, it generally does not take embossed detail or print particularly well. It is best to avoid stickers for labelling, as these can make it more difficult to recycle the product.

Reuse

Paper pulp mouldings provide limited opportunities for reuse.

Recycling

Because paper pulp is a cellulose-based fibrous material the mouldings can be recycled with paper and card.

Potential uses for recycled paper pulp mouldings

Paper pulp mouldings can be repulped with conventional paper and card to make more moulded pulp products (for example, egg boxes) or paper and card with recycled content, such as corrugated cardboard for transit packaging.

Lightweighting

Double-pressed trays with thinner walls and more detail are typically used as an alternative to vacuum formings to pack high-value items, such as mobile phones.

Biodegradability

Paper pulp mouldings are biodegradable.

Compostability

Paper pulp mouldings are compostable, both at home with garden waste or in an industrial composter, but packaging is often not accepted for industrial composting.

Landfill

Disposing of paper pulp mouldings in landfill sites is not environmentally friendly, as they biodegrade anaerobically and emit methane.

Bagasse food container

MOULDED BAGASSE PULP

➕ good-quality mouldings / can be used in conventional and microwave ovens / use of sugar-cane waste / recyclable

❗ sugar-cane production is linked to destruction of rainforests and pressure on food crops / high use of water and energy / GM crops may be used in its production

Typically used to manufacture

- **pots** *(see p. 213)*
- **trays** for fruit and vegetables *(see p. 217)*
- **burger boxes** *(see p. 222)*
- **disposable plates** and **cups**

Characteristics for packaging

Bagasse is the normally burned, fibrous remnants of sugar cane left over after the juice is extracted. It can be used to create a lightweight pulp product that takes surface detail much more faithfully than paper pulp, and is therefore excellent for containers with moulded lettering.

It takes heat well, so bagasse trays can be used in microwave ovens and in conventional ovens at temperatures up to around 200°C (390°F).

Sugar-cane production has been stepped up in South America to meet the need for the biofuel ethanol, which has led to a hastening of rainforest destruction for farmland. Additionally, there is no guarantee that GM crops have not been used in the production of bagasse, so the material raises some difficult questions. However, this does not mean that properly sourced bagasse cannot make a useful environmental contribution.

Manufacture

The pulp is typically moulded from slurry sprayed on to a drum that holds fine mesh moulds. It is sucked against the moulds and the mouldings are then dried. A finer finish and thinner walls can be achieved by using the double pressing (or hot pressing) method of manufacture where the pulp is squeezed into shape between two moulds.

Reuse

Moulded bagasse pulp is not reusable.

Recycling

Bagasse can be recycled with paper and card.

Potential uses for recycled bagasse

Bagasse can be pulped with conventional paper and card to make more moulded pulp products or recycled paper and card products.

Lightweighting

Moulded bagasse is a lightweight alternative to conventional paper pulp mouldings.

Biodegradability

Bagasse is biodegradable.

Compostability

Bagasse can be home composted and takes between one and six months to break down fully. Although it is industrially compostable, packaging is often not accepted for industrial composting.

Incineration

Incineration and energy recovery is a better and more practical option than landfill for bagasse pulp mouldings.

Landfill

Disposing of bagasse pulp mouldings in landfill sites is not environmentally friendly, as they biodegrade anaerobically and emit methane.

Palm-fibre tray

MOULDED PALM FIBRE

+ good-quality mouldings / makes use of palm-oil residue / recyclable

! palm-oil production is linked to the destruction of rainforests

Typically used to manufacture

- **trays** for fruit and vegetables *(see p. 217)*
- **burger boxes** *(see p. 222)*
- **pots** *(see p. 213)*
- **disposable plates** and **cups**

Characteristics for packaging

Palm fibres left over when palm oil is produced are used to create a pulp that takes surface detail well. Palm-oil production is often unregulated and has led to the destruction of Far Eastern rainforests, so it is important to verify the source of the material.

The long fibres give the moulded pulp good tensile strength, and it has a certain amount of natural moisture-resistance.

Manufacture

The pulp is typically moulded from slurry sprayed on to a drum that holds fine mesh moulds. It is sucked against the moulds and the mouldings are then dried. A finer finish and thinner walls can be achieved by using the double pressing (or hot pressing) method of manufacture where the pulp is squeezed into shape between two moulds.

Reuse

Moulded palm fibre is not reusable.

Recycling

Palm fibre can be recycled with paper and card.

Potential uses for recycled palm fibre

Palm fibre can be pulped with conventional paper and card to make more moulded pulp products or recycled paper and card products.

Lightweighting

Moulded palm fibre is a lightweight alternative to conventional paper pulp mouldings.

Biodegradability

Palm fibre is biodegradable and will break down within 90 days.

Compostability

Palm fibre can be home or industrially composted, but packaging is often not accepted for industrial composting.

Incineration

Incineration and energy recovery is a better and more practical option than landfill for palm-fibre mouldings.

Landfill

Disposing of palm-fibre mouldings in landfill sites is not environmentally friendly, as they biodegrade anaerobically and emit methane.

Brands

Earthcycle.

MOULDED BAMBOO FIBRE/PULP

✚ **abundant and fast growing / takes surface detail / recyclable**

❗ **threat to ancient bamboo forests and rainforests / unlike some other pulp materials that come into contact with food / bamboo is not waste material from another process**

Typically used to manufacture

- **trays** for fruit and vegetables *(see p. 217)*
- **burger boxes** *(see p. 222)*
- **disposable plates** and **cups**

Characteristics for packaging

Bamboo is a uniquely versatile material. It is fast growing and readily available, so is a practical alternative to paper pulp, and can be used in the same way. However, unlike paper pulp it is non-porous, which gives it more potential food-related uses.

Bamboo farms are major suppliers of the raw material, but it is important to check the source, as many bamboo forests are under threat. There is also some concern over bamboo grown on plantations, as many of these have come about through deforestation, which is destroying the habitat of many of China's indigenous species.

For pulp mills, bamboo is a popular alternative to softwood, as it can be used without the need to modify the pulping process.

Manufacture

Like paper pulp, bamboo pulp can be relatively easily moulded and takes fine surface details. It is typically moulded from slurry sprayed on to a drum lined that holds fine mesh moulds. It is sucked against the moulds and the mouldings are then dried. A finer finish and thinner walls can be achieved by using the double pressing (or hot pressing) method of manufacture where the pulp is squeezed between two moulds.

Reuse

Moulded bamboo pulp is not reusable.

Recycling

Bamboo pulp can be recycled with paper and card.

Potential uses for recycled bamboo pulp

Bamboo pulp can be pulped with conventional paper and card to make more moulded-pulp products or recycled paper and card products.

Lightweighting

Moulded bamboo pulp is a lightweight alternative to conventional paper-pulp mouldings.

Biodegradability

Bamboo pulp is biodegradable.

Compostability

Bamboo pulp can be home or industrially composted, but packaging is often not accepted for industrial composting.

Incineration

Incineration and energy recovery is a better and more practical option than landfill for bamboo pulp.

Landfill

Disposing of bamboo pulp mouldings in landfill sites is not environmentally friendly as they biodegrade anaerobically and emit methane.

Brands

Enviroarc.

Pulpcircle.

BIODEGRADABLE PLASTICS

BIODEGRADABLE PLASTICS ARE GENERALLY DESIGNED TO BREAK DOWN QUICKLY IN OUTDOOR CONDITIONS AND ARE SPECIFICALLY TARGETED AT PRODUCTS NORMALLY ASSOCIATED WITH LITTERING OR WHICH MAY HARM WILDLIFE.

Foamed starch chips

BIODEGRADABLE PLASTICS

➕ **biodegradable / no residue**

❗ **require specific conditions to break down / not as strong as additive-based conventional plastics / can potentially contaminate recycling stream**

Typically used to manufacture

- **food-tray lidding, overwrapping** (see p. 226 [films])
- **carrier bags** (see pp. 225-26)
- **beverage bottles** (see p. 207)
- **food trays** (see p. 216)

Characteristics for packaging

Although biodegradable plastics have many of the characteristics of conventional plastics, they theoretically break down completely in the environment after being consumed by micro-organisms.

Examples include PLA, and plastics made with cellulose and starch.

Manufacture

The manufacturing processes for bio-degradable plastic packaging are typically those used for conventional fossil-based plastics, such as thermoforming, extrusion, injection moulding and blow moulding. However, the functionality of the packaging is currently limited in comparison to that of the fossil plastics.

Reuse

Biodegradable plastics have limited opportunities for reuse. One of the most obvious is foamed starch chips.

Recycling

Some cellulose-based bioplastics are recyclable with paper. However, although other bioplastics are also recyclable, collection and identification remain major hurdles to widespread recycling.

Lightweighting

Biodegradable plastics provide some lightweighting opportunities, perhaps as alternatives to pulp packaging.

Biodegradability

Biodegradable plastics are broken down by the elements and are consumed by micro-organisms.

Compostability

Biodegradable plastics may be compostable, but packaging is not generally accepted for industrial composting.

Incineration

Incineration and energy recovery is a better and more practical option than landfill for biodegradable plastics.

Landfill

Disposing of biodegradable plastics in landfill sites is not environmentally friendly as they biodegrade anaerobically and emit methane.

HYDROLYTICALLY BIODEGRADABLE PLASTICS

+ **biodegradable / no residue**

! **susceptible to water damage / require specific conditions to break down / not as strong as additive-based conventional plastics / can potentially contaminate the recycling stream**

Typically used to manufacture

- **trays for chocolates** *(see p. 216)*
- **carrier bags** *(see pp. 225–26)*
- **wraps for newspapers** *(see p. 226 [films])*

Characteristics for packaging

Hydrolytically biodegradable plastics break down as a result of a chemical reaction with water. They are typically based on corn starch, potato starch or palm oil. Producing the oil contributes to the destruction of rainforests in Indonesia, so it is important to check the source of the plastic. PHA *(see p. 198)*, a bioplastic made by fermenting corn sugar or palm oil with micro-organisms that process plastics, is also water soluble.

The ability of hydrolytically biodegrable plastics to break down when they are in contact with water is also their Achilles heel, since they have to be restricted to low-moisture environments. However, development of these plastics is ongoing so the balance between degradability and durability is constantly improving.

Hydrolytically biodegradable plastics are often used as a medium for degrading conventional plastics.

Manufacture

Hydrolytically biodegradable plastics are generally used to make films, but some can be thermoformed, foamed or blow-moulded.

Reuse

Opportunities for reuse are limited. One of the most obvious is foamed starch chips.

Recycling

Hydrolytically biodegradable plastics are not recyclable.

Lightweighting

Hydrolytically biodegradable plastics provide some lightweighting opportunities.

Biodegradability

Hydrolytically biodegradable plastics start to biodegrade when they come into contact with water.

Compostability

Hydrolytically biodegradable plastics are theoretically compostable, but they may degrade quickly when exposed to the elements.

Incineration

Hydrolytically biodegradable plastics can be incinerated.

Landfill

Hydrolytically biodegradable plastics biodegrade anaerobically in landfill and emit methane, but they may degrade before reaching the site.

DEGRADABLE PLASTICS

DEGRADABLE PLASTICS ARE DESIGNED TO DEGRADE QUICKLY AS A RESULT OF BEING EXPOSED TO SPECIFIC ENVIRONMENTAL FACTORS, SUCH AS OXYGEN, WATER OR LIGHT, WHICH MAKE THEM 'DISAPPEAR', RATHER THAN REMAIN IN LANDFILL OR THE SEA FOR MANY YEARS. INCORPORATING AN ADDITIVE, SUCH AS STARCH, IN THE PLASTIC MASTERBATCH MAKES THEM BREAK UP INTO SMALL PIECES.

HYDROLYTICALLY DEGRADABLE PLASTICS

➕ **degradable / no visible residue**

❗ **fossil-based plastics are used in their production / require specific conditions to break down / can potentially contaminate the recycling stream**

Typically used to manufacture

- **carrier bags** *(see pp. 225–26)*
- **wraps for newspapers** *(see p. 226 [films])*
- **transit packaging** *(see pp. 231–32)*

Characteristics for packaging

Hydrolytically degradable plastics are conventional plastics, typically LDPE, which are blended with starch or another hydrolytically degradable material.

Manufacture

Hydrolytically degradable plastics are typically used to make films.

Reuse

Opportunities for reuse are limited, but there is no reason why a hydrolytically degradable carrier bag should not be reused.

Recycling

Hydrolytically degradable plastics are not recyclable.

Lightweighting

Hydrolytically degradable plastics tend to have lightweight applications.

Biodegradability

Hydrolytically degradable plastics are non-biodegradable.

Compostability

Hydrolytically degradable plastics are non-compostable.

Incineration

Hydrolytically degradable plastics can be incinerated.

Landfill

The conditions required for hydrolytically degradable plastics to break down may not be present when they are buried in landfill, but they are likely to have degraded before this happens.

OBPS *(OXO-[BIO]DEGRADABLE PLASTICS)*

➕ **degradable / may be recyclable / no perceptible residue**

❗ **fossil-based plastics are used in their production / require specific conditions to break down / may leave toxins in the soil / can potentially contaminate the recycling stream**

Typically used to manufacture

- **carrier bags** *(see pp. 225–26)*
- **wraps for newspapers** *(see p. 226 [films])*

Characteristics for packaging

Oxo-(bio)degradable plastics (OBPs) are made by adding chemicals to conventional plastics in the masterbatch. This reduces their molecular weight and increases the speed of oxidization (in air), which allows them to degrade in the soil – typically this takes from six months to five years, and is initiated by exposure to light. They are then consumed by micro-organisms in a few months to a few years, rather than hundreds of years. Manufacturers can control the speed of oxidation, so that the plastic does not start to degrade in-store. Because conventional plastics are used, OBPs are cheaper to produce than bioplastics.

However, there are doubts as to whether oxo-biodegradable plastics do anything more than degrade into extremely small pieces, and pass through the micro-organisms rather than being consumed by them. They are sometimes simply called oxo-degradable plastics.

One criticism of OBPs is that their performance is not always consistent with manufacturers' claims. There are also concerns that the conditions required for them to break down may not be present in the soil, and that the additives used in their production – manganese, cobalt and iron – could make them toxic.

Oxo-biodegradable plastics break down reliably when there is a supply of oxygen. They would, therefore, normally degrade if discarded as litter.

Manufacture

Currently OBPs are mainly used to make carrier bags and film for wrapping newspapers.

Reuse

Opportunies for reuse are limited. An obvious example is carrier bags.

Recycling

OBPs are held to be recyclable by their manufacturers, but the recycling industry has concerns that introducing degradable material to the recycling process weakens the finished recyclate. However, manufacturers claim that the active additives are quickly dispersed, and so have a negligible effect on any recyclate.

Lightweighting

OBPs tend to be used only for lightweight applications, typically as an alternative to conventional fossil-plastic films.

Biodegradability

OBPs are generally held to be degradable rather than biodegradable, but their manufacturers would dispute this.

Compostability

OBPs are non-compostable.

Incineration

OBPs can be incinerated.

Landfill

There is no guarantee that the conditions needed for OBPs to break down will be present in compacted landfill, where little oxygen may be available to start the process of degradation.

The packaging of your typical takeaway meal

PBPS *(PHOTO-[BIO]DEGRADABLE PLASTICS)*

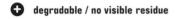 **+** degradable / no visible residue

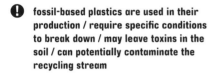 **!** fossil-based plastics are used in their production / require specific conditions to break down / may leave toxins in the soil / can potentially contaminate the recycling stream

Typically used to manufacture

- takeaway food packaging (see p. 222)
- carrier bags (see pp. 225–26)

Characteristics for packaging

Photo-biodegradable plastics (PDPs) are conventional plastics that are treated to start breaking down in sunlight. They are then consumed by micro-organisms in the same way as oxo-biodegradable plastics (see p. 192). The doubts about whether these plastics are digested by the micro-organisms also apply to PBPs.

PBPs are particularly suited to uses where the packaging might be discarded in the open, such as takeaway food packaging, and are sometimes combined with oxo-biodegradable plastics to enhance degradation.

Manufacture

PBPs are typically used to make films.

Reuse

Opportunities for reuse are limited, but PBP carrier bags are reusable.

Recycling

PBPs are held to be recyclable by their manufacturers, but recycling industry insiders maintain that introducing degradable material to the recycling process weakens the finished recyclate.

Lightweighting

PBPs are alternatives to conventional lightweight films and therefore tend to have lightweight applications.

Biodegradability

PDPs are generally held to be degradable rather than biodegradable, but their manufacturers would dispute this.

Compostability

PDPs are non-compostable.

Incineration

PBPs can be incinerated.

Landfill

The conditions required for PBPs to break down may not be present when they are buried in landfill.

BIOPLASTICS

BIOPLASTICS ARE DERIVED FROM CROPS, TYPICALLY MAIZE BUT ALSO PALM OIL, SUGAR CANE AND SOFTWOOD, AMONG OTHERS. CONTRARY TO POPULAR BELIEF, NOT ALL OF THEM ARE BIODEGRADABLE; SOME ARE IDENTICAL TO CONVENTIONAL PLASTICS.

AS A SUSTAINABLE ALTERNATIVE TO FOSSIL PLASTICS THEY ARE OFTEN HYPED AS BEING THE ANSWER TO ENVIRONMENTALISTS' PRAYERS. HOWEVER, NOT ONLY DO THE MAJORITY OF BIOPLASTICS LACK MANY OF THE QUALITIES THAT MAKE CONVENTIONAL PLASTICS SO INDISPENSABLE, THEY ALSO RAISE ALL SORTS OF UNCOMFORTABLE QUESTIONS ABOUT FARMING METHODS AND THE USE OF LAND FOR NON-FOOD CROPS.

Starch chips

STARCH

➕ **mouldable / compostable / usually hydrolytically biodegradable**

❗ **breaks down quickly, so uses can be limited**

Typically used to manufacture

- **transit packaging** (see pp. 231-32); loose-fill foamed chips (alternative to polystyrene foam)
- **burger boxes** (see p. 222)
- **base material** for more durable bioplastics
- **binding medium** for degradable bags

Characteristics for packaging

Starch is a natural enzyme that occurs as a result of photosynthesis in plants. Sources include maize, potatoes, cassava, wheat, soy, sugar cane, tapioca and rice.

It is not particularly durable in its raw form, and is vulnerable to moisture damage, but it can be processed into a variety of different plastics, both conventional and biodegradable. Starch is often combined with fossil-based plastics to allow them to degrade, and is frequently used as a binding medium for other materials.

PLA (see p. 197) is the most high-profile starch-based bioplastic, but its processing makes it far more durable than starch.

Manufacture

Starch can be thermoformed, injection-moulded, foamed or extruded as film.

Reuse

Opportunities for reuse are limited. An obvious example is foamed starch chips.

Recycling

Starch is not recyclable.

Lightweighting

As a plastic, starch has some lightweighting opportunities. It is often used as a binding medium for other materials.

Biodegradability

Starch biodegrades on contact with water.

Compostability

Starch is home and industrially compostable, but packaging is often not accepted for industrial composting.

Incineration

Starch can be incinerated.

Landfill

Starch emits methane in the anaerobic conditions of landfill, but in its unstable, raw form it is likely to degrade before it reaches the site.

Paperfoam moulded tray

PAPERFOAM

➕ biodegradable / robust / good surface detailing / recyclable with paper / lightweight

❗ hydrolytically biodegradable to some extent

Typically used to manufacture

- trays for CDs *(see p. 222)*
- transit packaging *(see pp. 231-32)*

Characteristics for packaging

Paperfoam is a hybrid of potato starch and wood fibre.

Manufacture

Paperfoam can be compression-moulded to create a surface finish that is far superior to that of moulded pulp, with an appearance more like plastic. It is ideally suited to presentation packaging as well as transit trays for cameras and mobile phones. As a structural material it is durable, and it is also recyclable and compostable, which makes it a compelling alternative for CD jewel cases.

Reuse

Paperfoam has great potential for reuse. The clearest current example is as CD cases.

Recycling

Paperfoam is recyclable with paper.

Potential uses for recycled paperfoam

Recycled paperfoam can be used in the same way as recycled paper and card.

Lightweighting

Paperfoam is a lightweight alternative to other structural materials.

Biodegradability

Paperfoam is biodegradable.

Compostability

Paperfoam is compostable, but packaging is often not accepted for industrial composting.

Incineration

Incineration is preferable to landfill for paperfoam.

Landfill

Disposing of paperfoam in landfill sites is not environmentally friendly, as it biodegrades anaerobically (without oxygen) and emits methane.

HIGH AMYLOSE CORN STARCH

➕ durable / readily compostable / mouldable / water soluble (hydrolytically biodegradable)

❗ biodegrades on contact with water / high land use / can potentially contaminate the recycling stream

Typically used to manufacture

- foam trays for chocolates, fruit and vegetables *(see p. 217)*
- biodegradable carrier bags *(see p. 226)*
- bagging films for fresh produce *(see p. 226 [films])*

Characteristics for packaging

The hybridized maize used to produce high amylose corn starch has a high amylose content and can be used as plastic resin without the need to blend it with other materials. High amylose corn starch biodegrades on contact with water.

Manufacture

High amylose corn starch is typically used for thermoformed sheets or film.

Reuse

High amylose corn starch is not suitable for reuse.

Recycling

If high amylose corn starch is used in biodegradable carrier bags they can contaminate the recycling stream.

Various forms of PLA

Lightweighting

High amylose corn starch is an alternative to lightweight fossil-based plastics.

Biodegradability

High amylose corn starch biodegrades on contact with moisture. This is its strength, but also its weakness because it can limit potential packaging uses.

Compostability

High amylose corn starch is home and industrially compostable, but packaging is often not accepted for industrial composting.

Incineration

Incineration and energy recovery is a better and more practical option than landfill for high amylose corn starch.

Landfill

Disposing of high amylose corn starch plastics in landfill is not environmentally friendly as they break down anaerobically and release methane.

Brands

Mater-Bi.

Plantic (hydrolytically degradable) labels, chocolate trays.

PLA (POLYLACTIC ACID)

➕ **extremely durable / mouldable / behaves like many fossil-based plastics**

❗ **not readily compostable / can easily contaminate conventional recycling streams / high land use / often uses GM crops**

Typically used to manufacture

- **films** *(see p. 226)*
- **clear bottles** *(see p. 207)*
- **dessert pots** *(see p. 213)*
- **resealable tubs** *(see p. 215)*
- **transit packaging**; foamed PLA *(see pp. 231–32)*
- **punnets** *(see p. 216)*
- **flow-wrap/carrier bags** *(see p. 225)*

Characteristics for packaging

Polylactic acid (PLA) is a clear plastic produced from fermented starch derived from sugar cane and maize (corn), which is converted to lactic acid. It is an extremely adaptable thermoplastic, with many of the properties of conventional plastics.

It does not degrade readily, so products made with PLA are fairly stable in most conditions. However, it is brittle and has a low melting point compared to conventional plastics.

PLA suffers from all the negative aspects of bioplastics in general, but it is potentially harmful in other ways, too. Its appearance and functionality allow it to compete directly against conventional plastics, but poor compostability compromises its environmental credentials. Worse still, if it is used for other types of normally recyclable packaging, such as clear bottles, it can easily contaminate conventional plastic recyclate, if recycled accidentally.

Given that it is promoted as a one-stop direct replacement for many conventional plastics it suits producers not to dwell on its questionable aspects. Instead the focus is almost entirely on its sustainability and supposed biodegradability.

Some environmentalists argue that PLA can be turned into fuel relatively easily, but, considering the difficulties associated with collection and sorting, energy recovery through incineration seems much more practical.

Manufacture

PLA can be injection-moulded, blow-moulded, foamed, vacuum-formed and extruded as a film.

Reuse

Although PLA is durable it is also brittle, so cannot yet compete equally with plastics. However, it is often used for lidded food pots, which are certainly strong enough to be reused.

Recycling

PLA is not usually collected for recycling: because it has a lower melting point than conventional plastics it can cause serious contamination if it is accidentally mixed with them.

Lightweighting

PLA is used as a replacement for lightweight conventional plastics.

Biodegradability

PLA is slow to degrade when conventional composting methods are used, and may potentially take many months, rather than weeks, to break down.

Compostability

Some film variants of PLA are compostable, but moulded products can only be industrially composted with the addition of water and heat – a sustained temperature of around 37°C (100°F) is required for PLA to be digested in an industrial composting facility. Windrow or ASP (aerated static pile) composting is not sufficient. In addition, packaging is often not accepted for industrial composting.

Incineration

Incineration and energy recovery is a better and more practical option than landfill for PLA.

Landfill

Disposing of PLA in landfill – its most likely destination – is not environmentally friendly as it breaks down anaerobically and emits methane.

Brands

Natureworks.

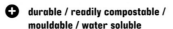

PHA *(POLYHYDROXYALKANOATE)* **AND PHB** *(POLYHYDROXYBUTYRATE)*

 durable / readily compostable / mouldable / water soluble

! **high cost / hydrolytic biodegradability can limit where PHA and PHB are used**

Typically used to manufacture

- **carrier bags** *(see pp. 225-26)*
- **films** *(see p. 226)*
- **bottles** *(see p. 207)*
- **yogurt pots** *(see p. 213)*

Characteristics for packaging

Polyhydroxyalkanoate (PHA) and polyhydroxybutyrate (PHB) are made by feeding sugars (usually corn) to engineered microbes inside fermentation tanks. The microbes convert the sugar into bioplastic.

Criticisms of PHA and PHB include the large amounts of energy required to produce them.

Manufacture

PHA and PHB have many of the properties of conventional plastics, and can be used for processes such as injection moulding, thermoforming, blow moulding and extrusion.

Reuse

Their reuse is limited because they biodegrade when they come into contact with water.

Recycling

PHA and PHB are not recyclable using current systems, and cause harmful contamination of recyclate if they are accidentally mixed in with conventional recycling streams.

Lightweighting

PHA and PHB are hydrolytically biodegradable alternatives to conventional lightweight plastics.

Biodegradability

PHA and PHB are biodegradable in contact with water or soil, and typically break down within two to three months.

Compostability

PHA and PHB are home and industrially compostable, but packaging is often not accepted for industrial composting.

Incineration

Incineration and energy recovery is a better and more practical option than landfill for PHA and PHB.

Landfill

Disposing of PHA and PHB in landfill – their most likely destination – is not environmentally friendly as they break down anaerobically and emit methane.

Brands

Mirel.

Sugar-cane crop – one of the feedstocks from which green polyethylene and Bio-PET can be made

GREEN POLYETHYLENE

➕ durable / easily recycled / same properties as conventional polypropylene

❗ high cost / high land use

Typically used to manufacture

- **bottles** *(see p. 207)* for beverages (milk), lubricants, etc
- **caps** *(see p. 230)*
- **films** *(see p. 226)*
- **carrier bags** *(see pp. 225-26)*

Green polyethylene effectively has the same chemical make-up as fossil-based plastics produced from ethane. This is normally obtained from naphtha (a petroleum derivative), but Braskem, a Brazilian manufacturer, pioneered the production of ethane from sugar-cane ethanol, which is usually grown for biofuel. Although the process is relatively efficient, the resultant plastic is costly compared with fossil-based plastics, but fluctuations in oil prices, plus the bioplastic tag, can make it extremely attractive.

Although green polyethylene is identical to the fossil plastic, it theoretically has a much-improved environmental profile. This is because much of the carbon dioxide it releases into the atmosphere (if incinerated) has only recently been absorbed by the sugar cane, rather than being emitted after millions of years stored underground.

There are, of course, several reasons why green polyethylene can be as environmentally unfriendly as conventional polyethylene, as well as additional factors related to bioplastic/fuel production.

- Farming the sugar-cane crop uses a great deal of fossil fuel, as does the industrial process to convert ethanol to ethane and plastics.
- Additives often do more harm to the environment than the base plastic.
- Biofuel/plastic crops in Brazil are contributing to destruction of the rainforest either directly or indirectly (by displacing other crops). However, the country's recent pledges to protect the climate are encouraging.

However, producers of biodegradable bioplastics should be concerned about green polyethylene. The future initially looked bright for them, despite the many arguments against their products. Then, just when they were starting to gain some ground in the near certainty that fossil-based plastics would more or less die out within a few decades, along came green polyethylene.

Because green polythene has the same chemical make-up as fossil plastics, it has an instant head start in usability, whereas biodegradables have a long way to go to match the performance of conventional plastics. Another major problem with biodegradable bioplastics is the need to separate them from conventional plastics in recycling systems.

One slightly alarming factor is the relish with which Braskem are setting about offering all the usual colour choices, pearlescents and metallics, rather than taking the opportunity to focus on making their material more usefully recyclable by keeping it clear.

Recently, there has been a great deal of interest in exploiting the potential of algae to produce ethanol for both fuel and plastics. Theoretically, this has the advantage that it would not divert food crops to fuel and plastic production.

Manufacture

Green polythene is used for processes including blow moulding, injection moulding, vacuum forming, extrusion and films.

Reuse

Because green polythene has the same properties as fossil-based plastics it can be reused in the same ways.

Recycling

A major advantage that green polythene has over biodegradable bioplastics is the ease with which it can be recycled with conventional plastics. Coca-Cola and Tetra Pak are trialling 'green' conventional plastics in their products.

Pile of sugar-cane in the field

Potential uses for recycled green polythene

Potential uses include blow-moulded bottles, car parts, garden furniture.

Lightweighting

Green polythene has good lightweighting potential.

Biodegradability

Green polythene is non-biodegradable.

Compostability

Green polythene is non-compostable.

Incineration

Incineration and energy recovery are a better and more practical option than landfill for green polythene.

Landfill

In the anaerobic conditions of landfill green polythene will take hundreds of years to degrade.

BIO-PET (POLYETHYLENE TEREPHTHALATE)

+ clear / from renewable sources / recylable / light / durable / low gas permeability / weldable

! high cost / high land use / brittle when blow moulded

Typically used to manufacture

- **clear bottles** for soft drinks and concentrates, sauces, toiletries, and detergents (see p. 207)

Characteristics for packaging

Bio-PET has the same chemical make-up as conventional PET, but is sourced from plant-based ethanol, typically from sugar cane. Like green polyethylene, it poses a problem for biodegradable bioplastics because it has the excellent functionality and recyclability of conventional PET. Unfortunately, it is also dependent on the high use of land, which affects other bioplastics. Nevertheless, bio-PET is gaining ground with high-profile manufacturers, such as Coca-Cola, Heinz and Danone (Volvic), all using bio-PET in some of their products.

Manufacture

Typically blow moulding, but sheet and film grades will become more commonplace.

Reuse

PET bottles are collected for reuse in some European countries. A deposit or tax is payable on PET bottles to help fund the scheme.

Recycling

Like PET, bio-PET can easily be recycled, mainly because it is usually collected in the form of bottles, and is normally clear, so colour variation in mixed recyclate is not an issue. It can be converted into rPET (recycled PET) and reused for bottles, cartons, punnets, clear thermoformed tubs and food trays or polyester fibre. Blue and green PET may also be collected for recycling, but other colour variants are unlikely to be converted into rPET.

Potential uses for recycled green polythene

Bio-PET bottles can be reprocessed into food-grade packaging, which is in considerable demand. Other potential uses include: fibre, tote bags, rPET bottles, fleece for clothing, training shoes, luggage, upholstery, furniture, carpets, fibrefill, industrial strapping, sheet, film, and automotive parts including luggage racks, fuse boxes, bumpers, grilles and door panels.

Lightweighting

Although brittle, bio-PET offers excellent opportunities for lightweighting.

Biodegradability

Bio-PET is effectively non-biodegradable, breaking down over hundreds of years.

The many uses of cellophane

CELLULOSE-BASED FILMS/ CELLOPHANE

 low cost / recyclable / compostable

 mainly limited to low-performance films / typically used to manufacture

Typically used to manufacture

- **clear film wraps** *(see p. 226)*
- **carton windows** *(see p. 209 [Cartons])*
- **clear labels** *(see p. 228)*
- **flow-wrap/carrier bags** *(see pp. 225-26)*

Characteristics for packaging

The oldest bioplastic, cellulose was first used industrially in 1870 to produce celluloid. It is the earth's most common organic compound, and arguably the most sustainable form of bioplastic, as it is commonly extracted from wood pulp or cotton.

Although corn starch- and PLA-based films are more high profile in environmentally friendly packaging, they are currently oversubscribed, so some manufacturers are switching to cellulose-based films, which are being developed with sophisticated barrier and print properties.

Manufacture

Cellophane is made by processing cellulose from trees (or other fibrous sources) into rayon using carbon disulphide. This is converted into cellophane by immersion in a series of acid baths. The process uses a range of noxious chemicals, which rather tarnish the material's environmental image.

Reuse

Opportunities for reuse are unlikely.

Recycling

Because cellulose comes from the same source as paper and card, it can often be recycled with them, particularly if it is laminated to cardboard.

Potential uses for recycled cellulose

Recycled cellulose can be repulped with conventional paper and card and used to make recycled paper and card products.

Lightweighting

Cellulose-based films are used as lightweight alternatives to fossil-based films.

Biodegradability

Cellulose biodegrades more effectively than many starch-based alternatives (such as PLA).

Compostability

Uncoated cellulose-based films are home compostable, and coated ones may be industrially compostable, but packaging is often not accepted for industrial composting.

Incineration

Incineration and energy recovery is a better and more practical option than landfill for cellulose products.

Landfill

Disposing of cellulose products in landfill sites is not environmentally friendly, as they biograde anaerobically and emit methane.

Brands

Natureflex.

Innovia Films.

Clarifoil.

Compostability

Bio-PET is non-compostable.

Incineration

PET is one of the least damaging plastics from an environmental point of view. If burned it combusts completely, creating only water and carbon dioxide.

Landfill

In the anaerobic conditions of landfill PET is protected from bacterial action, so will take hundreds of years to degrade. This is not necessarily a bad thing, because it is effectively inert in comparison to plant-based methane-producing materials.

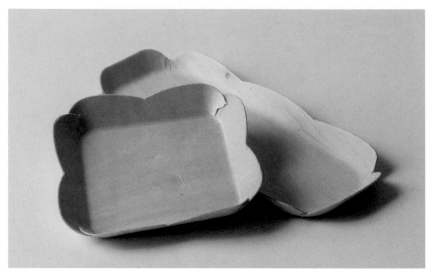

Wood trays

WOOD

➕ **strong / durable / projects quality / water resistant / natural / sustainable (depending on source)**

❗ **high cost compared to alternatives / lack of flexibility / limited printing options / weight / not usually recyclable**

Typically used to manufacture

- **crates**
- **cheese packaging**
- **presentation packaging** (see p. 228)
- **traditional packaging**, such as barrels
- **paper** and **card** (see pp. 172-77)
- **cellulose-based films** (see p. 226)

Characteristics for packaging

Although wood has largely been replaced by other materials it is still used for specific packaging applications, such as fruit crates and cheese boxes, and for all sorts of presentation packaging, particularly for premium spirits. The straight trunks of softwoods like spruce, which are still the primary source of fibre for paper, make them ideal for handling and processing.

Manufacture

The thin strips of wood used in cheese-box production are effectively peeled from the rotating tree trunk in large continuous sheets, in the same way that plywood is produced. The thicker sections of wood for fruit crates are sawn and planed to the correct thickness before being stapled together. Both processes are relatively easily mechanized, which reduces cost. Presentation packaging, by its nature, has to have a bespoke element, which often requires the use of hardwoods and more intricate machining and finishing. Wood can be moulded to some extent by steaming, or laminated into complex shapes.

Mouldable wood/plastic composites used in recycled garden furniture and some shipping pallets may potentially be used for more mainstream packaging.

Reuse

Wood provides more opportunities for reuse than many other materials, as its attractive grain gives it a unique quality. This may not apply so much to the very cheapest packs, but its finish and durability make wooden containers popular and practical to reuse.

Recycling

Wood is not usually accepted for kerbside recycling, but it can be converted into particle board or mixed with recycled plastics to create a mouldable, machinable wood plastic composite (WPC). This is both durable and long-lasting, and is therefore a popular choice for builders and furniture manufacturers.

Treated wood is less likely to be easily recyclable, so it is advisable to avoid heavy varnishes.

Potential uses for recycled wood

WPC building materials, such as decking, garden furniture, outdoor play equipment.

Lightweighting

Wood is not especially heavy relative to the amount used for applications such as fruit crates, and lightweighting is not a major concern.

Biodegradability

Wood is biodegradable.

Compostability

Wood is not compostable within a realistic timescale.

Incineration

Incinerating wood is sometimes considered to be carbon neutral as the carbon that is released has only recently been absorbed from the atmosphere. However, this does not take into account the carbon-emitting processes, such as farming, machining and transportation, involved in its manufacture.

Landfill

Wood emits methane in landfill.

OTHER MATERIALS

Many natural materials are being re-evaluated for their packaging potential, with varying success. One of the more interesting and engaging, but perhaps challenging, of these is the leaf of the Areca palm. The leaves are collected after they have been shed by the palm, and are moulded into attractive bowls and plates that retain distinctive leaf markings. They are not yet suitable for mainstream packaging, so in a sense they are a solution in search of an application.

New materials will demand lateral solutions, but biomaterials could become fertile ground for designers.

DIRECTORY
OF PACKAGING
FORMATS

BOTTLES AND JARS

Typical materials:

- **aluminium** *(see p. 167)*
- **glass** *(see p. 162)*
- **plastic –** HDPE, PET, rPET, PVC, PP, PS, LDPE *(see pp. 150-60)*
- **bioplastics –** PLA, PHA, PHB, green polythene *(see pp. 194-203)*
- **biodegradable plastics** *(see pp. 186-89)*

BOTTLES – ALUMINIUM

Aluminium bottles are a relatively new development in packaging. They allow a certain amount of customization of the form and are fully printable, with a range of closure options.

They are expensive to produce, compared with other bottle formats, but costs are coming down as new manufacturing techniques are developed.

BOTTLES/JARS – GLASS

Since the early 1980s glass has effectively been usurped by PET for bottling carbonated drinks. However, unlike PET it is impermeable and does not taint the product, and it remains the material of choice for wine, beer, spirit and olive bottles, as well as jars for food products. An advantage of glass bottles is that they can be filled at high temperatures, which allows more effective pasteurization. Unlike many plastic bottles, glass bottles are not moulded at the filling plant, so are transported empty to be filled.

The current focus on lightweighting glass to improve its environmental profile tends to limit the palette of bottle shapes to more rounded profiles, but the advantages are clear – as Coca-Cola demonstrated when they lightweighted their standard bottle and shaved 20 per cent off the weight. Lightweighting is not always this successful and can lead to increased breakages.

It is crucial to consult the bottle manufacturer at the start of a project, as their input is crucial in developing lightweighted structures.

BOTTLES – PLASTIC

Plastic bottles, derived from petrochemicals, have several advantages over glass bottles: they are cheap to produce, very little energy is used to manufacture them (compared with glass) and they are light (conserving energy in transportation) and strong. Up to 40 per cent less fuel is used to transport drinks in plastic bottles compared to glass ones. The production of plastic bottles accounts for around one-third of one per cent of total crude-oil usage.

The bottles are extremely practical and flexible from the design and retailing point of view. They are relatively easily recycled and, more importantly, effective systems are in place allowing them to be reprocessed with relative ease.

Plastic bottles are usually made from PET or HDPE, and sometimes PP or PVC. PP takes surface detail well, but is not always widely recyclable, so does not have the environmental advantages of PET or HDPE. The eventual reusability of plastic bottles depends on their colour (or lack of it). To be eligible for reprocessing into food-grade packaging they must be clear or translucent (the most common qualities for drinks bottles) or only slightly tinted.

Bottles for products such as toiletries, detergents and lubricants are moulded in a variety of colours, which means they are unlikely to be reprocessed because of the difficulties involved in controlling the resultant colour. Another variable in recycling coloured bottles is the effect of additives used to create special effects, such as pearlescence and metallics.

Many manufacturers mould plastic bottles on the site where they are filled, in hole-in-the-wall operations. This is environmentally preferable to delivering the bottles ready-moulded, which is effectively expending energy to transport air.

PLASTIC JARS

Blow-moulded plastic jars tend to be made from PET, HDPE and PVC, and are relatively easily recycled. Injection-moulded jars, used for cosmetics in particular, can be made from a wide variety of plastics, including PS, PET and PP, and recycling them is often challenging.

AEROSOLS

Typical materials:

- **aluminium** *(see p. 167)*
- **steel** *(see p. 169)*

AEROSOLS – ALUMINIUM

Aluminium aerosols are lighter than their steel counterparts and usually offer more opportunity for sculptural form. They are widely recyclable, and the propellant, product residue and plastics can be reclaimed.

AEROSOLS – STEEL

Steel aerosols are usually straight-sided, with a crimp-on top and base.

They are widely recyclable, and the propellant, product residue and plastics can be reclaimed.

CARTONS

Typical materials:

- **cardboard** *(see p. 174)*
- **plastic** – PET (PETG or APET), LDPE, PVC, PP *(see pp. 150-60)*
- **paper** *(see p. 174)*

CARTONS – CARDBOARD

Cardboard cartons provide copious graphic potential, and although their Achilles heel could be their opacity in relation to plastic alternatives, there are many ways to transcend the standard window format. Often there is no need for the plastic film, which not only prevents the customer interacting with the product, but also makes it more difficult to recycle the carton. An unusual position for the window, perhaps cutting into a corner, rings the changes and adds interest without increasing cost.

As with many other packaging formats, great efforts are being made in the area of lightweighting. Carton-grade cardboard is constructed in several layers, which might include a lightweight core sandwiched between denser outer layers suited to printing. The resulting material has similar structural and graphic properties to conventional carton boards, but with substantial weight savings. Other boards may use a high recycled content between printable outer layers.

When cellulose windows are used on a carton the board can often be recycled or composted without removing the windows, as cellulose (a bioplastic) is a major constituent of wood pulp. Metallic and plastic card laminates are unlikely to be conventionally recyclable.

CARTONS – PLASTIC SHEET

PET, RPET, PVC, PP

PET cartons are usually used as presentation or gift packaging. They display the product extremely well, are structurally strong and can be relatively cheap to originate, compared with clam packs. However, they are expensive compared with cartons made from cardboard, or from PVC, which is environmentally questionable.

PET cartons are not widely recyclable, and a more environmentally friendly option is to use recycled PET (rPET). Clear or frosted polypropylene (PP) cartons are another alternative, but they tend to have thicker walls than PET ones.

PET, rPET, PVC and PP may not be recyclable in their sheet form.

BEVERAGE CARTONS – MULTILAYER POLYCARD (PAPER, LDPE FOIL) CONSTRUCTION

Drinks cartons are multilayer constructions which are usually based on paperboard, aluminium foil and/or plastic film. They are becoming widely recyclable: Tetra Pak, in particular, have invested heavily in developing recycling facilities. Drinks cartons have several other environmental benefits. Because their footprint is square they are extremely space-efficient compared with round bottles, and can be suitable for hot filling and high-speed production. They are mainly comprised of paper, which is primarily from managed sources (or part recycled), and will biodegrade in landfill.

The cartons are constructed from huge rolls of laminated material, which is formed and welded to create them as they are filled. Unlike much bottle- and can-packing there is no need to transport empty containers to the filling plant. Pack manufacture and filling is a continuous seamless process.

CANS

Typical materials:

- **aluminium** *(see p. 167)*
- **steel** *(see p. 169)*

BEVERAGE CANS – ALUMINIUM

Aluminium cans for drinks are lightweight (and getting lighter), inexpensive and widely recyclable. The thickness of the wall is often less than that of a human hair, so the cans are an environmentally efficient form of packaging, although it could be argued that aluminium production in general is not exactly green.

The manufacturing process is inflexible, so the use of graphics is the only way to create brand differentiation.

BEVERAGE CANS – STEEL

As with aluminium cans, manufacturing steel cans for drinks is an inflexible process, so product differentiation can only be achieved by pack graphics. Vertical seaming is less common nowadays for beverage cans, but can be used to create more sculptural shapes and surface detail, albeit using heavier gauge steel.

Standard steel cans are heavier than their aluminium counterparts, but it is extremely easy to separate them from household waste with electromagnets, so the recovery rate is high.

FOOD CANS – STEEL

Although canned food lost out to frozen food in the 1950s and 1960s, the effectiveness of steel cans and tins at preserving foods for long periods, often without preservatives, means they remain an ever-popular and efficient form of packaging. They are retortable, relatively lightweight, easily handled and easily recycled. Steel allows a certain amount of variation in sculptural form, with a wide variety of different footprints: Heinz recently experimented with a square can for baked beans.

Steel cans are not associated with freshness, and to a certain extent they have been replaced by other materials. For example, soups come in a variety of different containers, such as pouches (doy bags), cartons and moulded plastic tubs or bottles.

TINS
(STORAGE/PRESENTATION)

Typical materials:

- **steel** *(see p. 169)*

Steel tins are often used for presentation packaging, typically as containers for biscuits or caddies for tea or coffee, and usually contain an airtight pack. They are potentially reusable, but despite this they eventually end up being recycled or landfilled, so in many cases they can be seen as no more than additional unnecessary packaging.

Steel tins can be recycled and are readily removed from the household waste stream with electromagnets. They are easily identified by their vertical seam and rolled edges at the base.

POUCHES (DOY BAGS) /SACHETS

Typical materials:

- **LDPE, PET, PP** *(see pp. 150–60)*
- **aluminium** *(see p. 167)*

Doy bags are a lightweight alternative to cans and bottles. They lend themselves to packing fresh foods, and use clear, multilayer plastics and aluminium foil where longer shelf life is needed. Their excellent graphic potential, along with their barrier properties, have made them extremely popular.

Aluminium pouches take up far less space than the steel cans and PET bottles they routinely replace, are considerably lighter and less energy is used to retort their contents. This means that despite being hard to recycle they make considerable energy savings over more traditional forms of packaging.

Sachets use similar materials and some of their uses are similar, but they are more likely than pouches to contain beauty as well as food products.

Given the same kind of investment manufacturers of beverage cartons have made in developing recycling facilities, aluminium pouches and sachets could be potentially recoverable on a large scale. However, the cost and energy consumption are currently prohibitive.

From an environmental point of view, it must be remembered that if the packs are destined for the chiller cabinet they will consume much more energy in-store than equivalent ambient foods.

POTS

Typical materials:

- ceramic
- **bioplastics** – PLA, PHA, PHB
  (see pp. 194-203)
- **plastic** – PS, LPDE *(see pp. 150-60)*
- **paper** *(see p. 174)*
- **moulded pulp** *(see p. 182 [bagasse], p. 183 [palm fibre])*

CERAMIC POTS

Ceramics – pottery and stoneware – predate glass as a packaging material. They have been used for thousands of years for amphorae, bottles and pots for storing food, and were replaced only in the early twentieth century. They are still used for speciality foods, such as mustard, jams and cider vinegar, usually to create an antique or rustic image.

Pottery and stoneware are relatively heavy and energy-hungry and, although they are not conventionally recyclable, they are robust and reusable. When they reach the end of their useful lives they are inert, with no stored energy, and simply become hardcore.

DESSERT POTS (YOGURT POTS, ETC) – VACUUM-FORMED PLASTIC

Foil-sealed vacuum-formed plastic pots are a high-speed packaging format that uses minimal materials to create hermetically sealed products. They are usually made from PS (polystyrene). PLA is the bioplastic alternative, but it is not compostable within realistic timescales or recyclable, and emits methane in landfill.

Additional card sleeves are not necessary in most cases, so should be avoided where possible.

DESSERT POTS – PAPER/LPDE

Dessert pots are often made from lightweight plastic and wrapped in paperboard to give the impression of traditional, waxed-cardboard punnets. While this suggests quality and environmental responsibility, the two materials are not easily separated, so it is not usually practical to recycle them. The waxed-cardboard-style pot is still used, but is usually no more recyclable than the wrapped plastic version, as it is in reality a paper/plastic laminate.

RESEALABLE TUBS

Typical materials:

- **plastic** – PLA, PP, rPET *(see pp. 150-60)*
- **paper** *(see p. 174)*

RESEALABLE TUBS – PLASTIC (INJECTION MOULDED)

Plastic tubs moulded in PP (polypropylene), with anti-tamper, watertight, resealable lids are an effective format for packing fresh foods from biscuits to soups. Because they are usually preprinted, require minimal equipment for assembly and can be hot-filled, they are well suited to smaller producers.

As PP is not widely recycled (although this varies by country) plastic tubs can have a poor environmental profile. To some extent it could be argued that they can be reused, but this may only postpone their destiny as landfill unless using them means that another purchase, for example of freezer containers, is unnecessary.

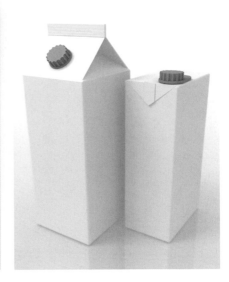

RESEALABLE TUBS - PLASTIC (THERMOFORMED)

Thermoformed tubs come in a variety of plastics, which means they are often not collected for recycling, as sorting them is difficult. Food contact can also be an issue.

Recycled PET (rPET) is a more environmentally friendly option and is suitable for clear tubs.

PLA, a bioplastic, may be used for moulded tubs but its barrier properties are not as good as those of conventional plastics.

FOILS

Typical materials:

- **aluminium** *(see p.167)*

Aluminium foils laminated to paperboard or plastic films are most often used to help preserve food and beverages. In particular, they have excellent gas barrier properties, which make them ideal for longlife or fresh produce that may otherwise have to be packed in heavier containers, such as glass. They are typically used for bags/pouches/ sachets, lidding for foods, pharmaceuticals, cosmetics, etc., beverage cartons and spiral-wound tubes for dry food.

Packaging that uses lightweight laminated films containing foil is difficult to recycle and collecting it is not usually considered cost-effective. Gable-top beverage cartons contain foil and can be recycled in some countries, as carton manufacturers have invested heavily in dedicated recycling facilities.

Heavier-gauge foils used for pie cases and takeaway foods are not laminated so can readily be recycled, but the availability of recycling for this type of aluminium alloy is not as widespread as it is for recycling aluminium cans.

TRAYS/ PUNNETS

Typical materials:

- **aluminium** *(see p. 167)*
- **plastic** – PS, LDPE, PP, rPET *(see pp. 150–60)*
- **biodegradable plastics** *(see p. 186 [biodegradable], p. 188 [hydrolytically biodegradable plastics])*
- **moulded pulp** *(see p. 180 [recycled paper pulp], p. 182 [bagasse], p. 183 [palm fibre], p. 184 [bamboo])*
- **high amylose corn starch** *(see p. 196)*
- **PLA** *(see p. 197)*

TRAYS – ALUMINIUM AND FOIL

Aluminium trays with foil lids require less packing equipment than the steel tins they sometimes replace, but they are more expensive. They are also lighter and potentially offer better graphic opportunities with fully printable lids. The lidding process is often done in combination with inert gas to preserve the product longer in the chiller cabinet. The packs are retortable and are therefore suitable for meat products, such as pet foods.

Aluminium trays are also used for raw foods prepared for roasting in the oven. They can be sealed with multilayer plastic film, so that the product is visible. The film is removed before the tray is placed in the oven.

Aluminium trays and foil are not made of the same alloy as aluminium cans, so cannot be reprocessed with them. If they are collected for recycling they are likely to be turned into components for the car industry.

TRAYS – FOAM PLASTIC, USUALLY EXPANDED PS/ STYROFOAM

Foam trays are increasingly used for packing fruit and vegetables. These generally need no protection, although it can be argued that it is necessary for fleshier fruits. Their especially good insulation properties means they are often used for raw meat and shrink film protects the product from contamination. They are an effective form of packaging in supermarkets, but would not be used or needed at a high-street butcher.

Foam trays are not widely recyclable, but there are several sustainable alternatives, including foamed starch, paper pulp and moulded paper.

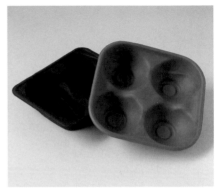

TRAYS/PUNNETS – PLASTIC (THERMOFORMED OR INJECTION-MOULDED)

Film-sealed plastic trays are lightweight and tend to be used for ready- or microwavable meals. They use packing equipment similar to that used for aluminium tray sealers and can contain inert gases to keep food fresh.

A range of plastics, including hydrolytically biodegradable plastics and multilayer plastics, are used and the trays can be thermoformed or injection-moulded. rPET is a more environmentally friendly option. Although some of the plastics are recyclable, many local authorities do not collect this type of packaging. It is bulky and hard to sort, so retrieving it is often not practical from both the cost and environmental point of view. Food contact also presents difficulties for recyclers, so any recycling is usually to low-grade materials.

This type of pack often features a cardboard wrap purely for graphics and pack information. Although this is recyclable, it is an extravagant use of materials so should be reduced to the minimum. Graphics can, for instance, be printed on the film lidding.

Punnets for fruit and vegetables are sealed with a clear plastic bag or shrink sleeving. This offers an opportunity to use bioplastics for both punnet and bag, provided there is no danger of either the punnets or film being recycled: bioplastics generally emit methane in landfill.

High amylose corn starch degrades in contact with water and has been used for low-moisture niche applications, such as vacuum-formed trays for chocolates.

TRAYS – PULP/CARD

A shrink-sleeved or bagged recyclable moulded pulp or card tray is a more sustainable alternative to a plastic punnet, unless weight or contamination have to be taken into account.

MODIFIED-ATMOSPHERE PACKAGING

Modified-atmosphere packaging (MAP) is gas-flushed, typically with nitrogen, oxygen or carbon dioxide. This removes most of the air around food, which prevents attack by aerobic microbes and increases shelf life. MAP is often used in conjunction with pasteurization techniques to further delay the action of bacteria.

Gas flushing is extremely important in the production of many fresh foods, including ready meals, potato crisps, meat products, sauces, soups, salads, confectionery and fresh pasta. When it is combined with refrigeration it can enable fresh foods to last for months without the use of preservatives. This reduces the amount of food waste going to landfill where it emits methane and simplifies the logistics of food transportation.

Gas flushing and refrigeration have made it viable to market previously unthinkable forms of fresh produce from around the world, but inevitably there is a point at which producers push the boundaries to the limit, enabling freshness and choice but also creating food waste from the most sensitive produce, such as prepared vegetables and salads. Not only does the wasted food emit methane in landfill, but all the other greenhouse-gas emissions along the production and supply chain will have been created for no good reason. While MAP undoubtedly improves the quality and longevity of food, it also contributes to supermarkets' reliance on energy-consuming chiller cabinets and refrigerated transport.

Shelf-life Extension with MAP

Numbers represent days of refridgerated shelf-life

Product	Non-MAP	MAP
Fresh red meat (high O2)	2-3	6-10
Fresh red meat (low O2)	2-3	21
Fresh sausage	4-5	15-16
Fresh processed poultry	3-10	12-18
Cooked poultry	5-16	21-30
Cooked/cured meats	1	30-45
Cheese	7	180+
Fresh Pasta	3	60+

Ref. Coextruded Plastic Technologies Inc.

BLISTER/CLAM PACKS

Typical materials:

- **plastic** – PET, PVC, APET
  (see pp. 150–60)
- **card** *(see p. 174)*

VACUUM FORMINGS

Vacuum formings are an extremely adaptable, but not usually recyclable, form of packaging. They are cheap, lightweight, robust and easily handled.

In PET and PVC they offer exceptional visibility and sculptural opportunity. However, PVC is environmentally questionable and should be avoided.

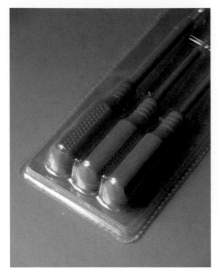

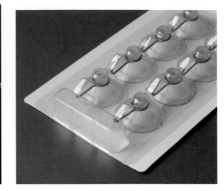

WELDED UHF OR RF (RADIO FREQUENCY) BLISTERS

Double-sided, welded plastic blister packs are extremely popular for electronic goods, gadgets and toys. They display the product well, and dynamic sculptural forms and complex graphic inserts can be used to add interest. All the elements in a product can be encapsulated and revealed by the blisters, without the need for additions such as wire ties.

This type of packaging is usually moulded in PVC or APET and (apart from the paper element) is not widely recyclable. The pack is often out of proportion to the product, in effect shipping air. Imaginatively designed card cartons with windows can be just as effective and more environmentally friendly.

CLAM PACKS

Clam packs are a high-visibility format that is often stapled or taped shut, and are used for a wide variety of products. They are usually moulded from PVC or APET and are not widely recyclable. The graphic area tends to be limited, either on an insert or a sticker, so the packs are mainly used on utility products and, increasingly, for delicate foods. However, using them for produce such as meringues and croissants, which could be packaged more sympathetically, is questionable.

CARD AND BLISTER

Card and blister packs have a card backing board for graphics and a plastic vacuum forming, usually PVC or PET, to hold the product. While they are not the most imaginative pack format, the card is often from sustainable sources and can be recycled or composted.

The plastic element could be removed by using an all-card solution, where the product is retained by the card. Some battery packaging works this way.

Opposite:
LDPE six-pack tie

SIX-PACK HOLDERS

Typical materials:

- **plastic** – LDPE *(see p. 158)*

From a materials perspective six-pack holders are a minimal, efficient and effective way of presenting a multipack of beverage cans. They are a good example of how designers need to think beyond simple materials reduction and consider how their choices can effect the environment in other ways. For example, discarded six-pack holders can be particularly hazardous to wildlife. This type of packaging is unlikely to be recycled, so six-pack holders are currently often made of degradable LDPE.

The alternatives are film shrink-wrap or a card sleeve, both of which seem extravagant compared with LDPE, but card has the advantage that it is recyclable and compostable, and is less of a hazard to wildlife.

MOULDED PULPS

Typical materials:

- **recycled paper pulp** *(see p. 180)*
- **moulded bagasse pulp** *(see p. 182)*
- **moulded palm fibre** *(see p. 183)*
- **moulded bamboo fibre/pulp** *(see p. 184)*

Moulded paper pulp has an overall environmental profile similar to that of card. It is most often seen as egg boxes, and increasingly as transit packaging for electronic products. It is also used for more creative packaging, which can include fine detailing and embossed lettering.

Consumers are usually positive about pulp packaging, but it tends to be heavy and space-consuming compared to plastic alternatives.

BURGER BOXES

Typical materials:

- **plastics** – PS *(see p. 160)*
- **biodegradable plastics** *(see p. 195 [starch])*
- **moulded pulp** *(see p. 180 [recycled paper pulp], p. 182 [bagasse], p. 183 [palm fibre], p 184 [bamboo])*

The classic insulating foamed plastic (PS) burger box is becoming a thing of the past. In response to environmental concerns about littering and the threat to wildlife and marine life, global manufacturers are opting for printed card. However, there are alternatives to PS, including biodegradable foamed starch materials and pulp mouldings.

VACUUM SKIN PACKAGING *(VSP)*

Typical materials:

- **card** *(see p. 174)*
- **plastic shrink-film compounds**

Vacuum skin packaging effectively bonds a layer of film to a backing card, and traps the product between the two layers. It keeps the product visible, but is a lowest common denominator form of unattractive, cheap packaging. It also renders the card unrecyclable.

TUBES

Typical materials:

- **card** *(see p. 174)*
- **plastic** – PET, rPET, PP, HDPE, LDPE, PVC *(see pp. 150–60)*
- **aluminium** *(see p. 167)*

SPIRAL-WOUND TUBES

Spiral-wound tubes are a robust form of card packaging. They are typically the central support for rolls of tissue or postal tubes, and are also used for powdered products, such as flour or cocoa.

Because they are paper-based their environmental profile is potentially good, but tubes lined with aluminium foil are unlikely to be recyclable or compostable, so will be landfilled and emit methane as they degrade.

FLEXIBLE PLASTIC TUBES

Flexible tubes for toiletries and creams are made from a variety of plastics, including PP, HDPE, LDPE and PVC. This makes it difficult to identify specific plastics, so plastic tubes are unlikely to be recycled at present.

Although doy bags are non-recyclable they are often more efficient than tubes, and tottles (inverted bottles) are a more recyclable option.

CLEAR PRESENTATION TUBES

PET or PVC tubes with end caps are most commonly used for gift packaging, and often hold the product in an internal fitment. PVC should certainly be avoided, but even PET tubes are not necessarily recyclable. Recycled PET (rPET) may be an option to improve the environmental impact.

BAGS

Typical materials:

- **LDPE, HDPE, PET, PP**, etc
- **Alufoil**
- **degradable and biodegradable plastics** *(see p. 192 [oxo-(bio)degradable plastics], p. 188 [hydrolytically biodegradable plastics], p. 191 [hydrolytically degradable plastics], p. 193 [photo-biodegradable plastics])*
- **bioplastics** – cellulose, PLA, PHA, PHB, green polythene *(see pp. 194–203)*

FLOW-WRAP BAGS: FORM, FILL AND SEAL

Flow-wrap – form, fill and seal bags – are lightweight, strong and energy-efficient, with good graphic potential. They are usually made with plastic film (PET, PP, LDPE, HDPE). The bags are often laminated in layers which makes recycling them impractical. They are typically used for products such as sweets, potato crisps and freezer bags, and are seamed from flat printed sheet, filled and then sealed in one continuous operation.

Aluminium foil is also used to make the bags and has the best barrier qualities. A recent study into the migration of mineral oils from ink residue in recycled cardboard into bagged food showed that only Alufoil bags prevented contamination.

CARRIER BAGS

Single-use, disposable carrier bags are widely acknowledged to harm marine life and are perceived as a waste of resources. As a result, heavy-duty reusable plastic bags (LDPE), and cotton and non-woven PP bags have been promoted as environmentally sound alternatives. However, a recent United Kingdom Environment Agency study entitled Life Cycle Assessment of Supermarket Carrier Bags found that this perception does not always match the reality. A cotton bag would have to be reused approximately 130 times before it became as environmentally efficient as a single-use bag. If the 'single-use' bag were reused just three times as a shopping bag the cotton bag would have to be reused 393 times to achieve the same carbon footprint. The figures for the heavy-duty LDPE and non-woven PP bags are much more realistic, with a reuse of four and 11 times respectively to achieve the same carbon footprint. Nevertheless, the single-use bag is arguably one of the best performing packaging formats in the study.

TYPE OF CARRIER	HDPE bag no secondary use	HDPE bag 40.3% reused as bin liners	HDPE bag 100% reused as bin liners	HDPE bag Used 3 times
Paper bag	3	4	7	9
LDPE bag	4	5	9	12
Non-woven PP bag	11	14	26	33
Cotton bag	131	173	327	393

The figures in the first column show the number of times each type of bag has to be reused to achieve the same carbon footprint as an HDPE carrier bag, then how reusing the single-use bag affects the efficiency of the other formats.

The typical supermarket carrier bag is generally HDPE, but it is also often made with recycled or degradable material, usually oxo-(bio)degradable plastics or starch-based degradable plastics such as hydrolytically degradable plastics, which are marketed as addressing littering and damage to marine life. There is some truth to this but critics argue that providing degradable bags encourages litter: even when the bags reach landfill they are easily blown in the wind and are more likely to end up in waterways than many other forms of packaging.

The degradable and biodegradable bags are not practically recyclable (although recyclability claims are made for bags made from oxo-[bio]degradable plastics).

FILMS

Typical materials:

- **plastics**: PET, PVC, HDPE, LDPE, PP, hydrolytically biodegradable plastics, oxo-(bio)degradable plastics *(see pp. 150-60)*
- **bioplastics**: cellulose, PLA, high amylose corn starch, PHA, PHB, green polythene *(see pp. 194-203)*

Plastic packaging films, often laminated in layers, lightweight and difficult to sort, are usually not practical to recycle. Despite this they are strong and energy-efficient, with good graphic potential and high barrier performance. They tend to be used for bagging fresh produce, food-tray lidding, overwrap, wraps for newspapers, carton windows, shrink-sleeving and labelling.

The impracticality of recycling plastic films makes bioplastic versions a potential alternative, especially for less demanding applications, such as salad bagging and for carton windows. Because films are less likely to reach the recycling stream there is less danger that changing to bioplastics would cause contamination. However, their likely destination is landfill, where they will emit methane as they degrade.

Bioplastic alternatives include cellulose and PLA.

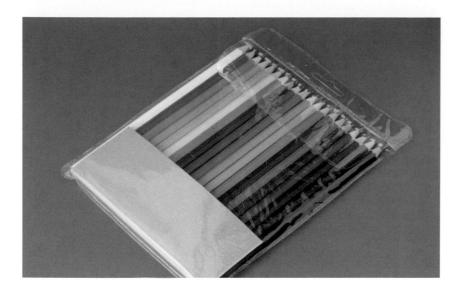

FLEXIBLE WALLETS

Typical materials:

- **plastic** – PVC *(see p. 156)*

Although PVC is an environmental nightmare, it does have some characteristics that cannot be mimicked by other materials, such as PET (which is so successful at replacing it for beverage bottles). The advantages of flexible PVC include high clarity, durability and flexibility, which make it a popular material for reusable (secondary use) packaging, such as cases for coloured crayons. However, it is hard to justify packing curtains or duvet covers – and many other products – in PVC wallets, as there is usually an alternative packaging format that does not create dubious after-uses.

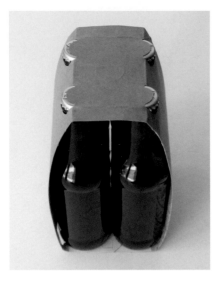

SLEEVES/ ENVELOPES

Typical materials:

- **card** (see p. 174)

Card sleeves are often used to add graphics and information to difficult-to-label packaging, particularly ready-meals in trays. However, they are also used simply to make a strong shelf impression or to differentiate a product from its competitors. Card sleeves on multipacks of yogurt, for instance, are entirely superfluous; it would be far better to make the pots an interesting shape and print on the lids. Similarly, film-sealed trays for ready-meals or cuts of meat could do without card sleeves, as any text or graphics could be printed on the sealing film.

The card may well be recyclable and compostable, but inevitably a large proportion will end up in landfill, where it will degrade anaerobically and emit methane.

Card envelopes do a similar job to sleeves, but are sometimes used to make high-quality foods, such as smoked salmon, appear more premium by covering cheaper-looking film-vacuum packaging.

LABELS/ SWING TAGS

Typical materials:

- **card** (see p. 174)
- **paper** (see p. 174)
- **cellulose** (see p. 201)

Self-adhesive labels can be a cost-effective way of applying graphics to hard-to-print surfaces or differentiating between products in a range without reprinting the whole pack. They are not usually recyclable or compostable, because of their high glue content, and should be easily removable from the rest of the product packaging so that it can be recycled more efficiently. However, there is a growing range of compostable adhesives, which can improve the environmental profile of self-adhesive labels to some extent.

The waxy backing paper on the labels is not conventionally recyclable. There are alternatives, such as linerless labels. These may be no better for recycling, but generate significantly less waste.

Swing tags are a minimal way of applying essential graphics to durable goods, such as clothes and kitchenware, that do not need other protection in-store. They are potentially both cost-effective and environmentally sound, but all too often they are made from non-recyclable plastics or feature pointlessly extravagant cords.

CLOSURES

Typical materials:

- **cork** (see p. 229)
- **aluminium** (see p. 167)
- **steel** (see p. 169)
- **plastic** – PP, LDPE, HDPE (see pp. 150–60)
- **bioplastics** – green polythene (see p. 199)

CORKS

Synthetic corks use a variety of plastic compounds and have replaced a large percentage of natural corks for low- to mid-range wines – an environmental story in itself.

Natural cork is the bark of the cork oak and is harvested every ten years in a process that does not damage the tree. The cork forests of the western Mediterranean are a complex, managed ecosystem that has developed over thousands of years, and play a major role in preventing desertification. The widespread introduction of plastic corks has threatened the traditional cork industry and the maintenance of the forests, with potentially dire consequences for local communities.

Synthetic corks are cheap, cannot taint the wine and are easily removed from the bottle without disintegrating, but they are really only suitable for wines that do not mature in the bottle. Natural corks are much better at allowing the wine to breathe and mature within the bottle, but are susceptible to cork taint. They are, however, compostable.

The producers of synthetic corks argue that the natural cork industry did not have the capacity to sustain current levels of demand, as cork oaks have to grow for up to 40 years before their bark can be stripped. Synthetic corks are not recyclable.

CLOSURES – METALLIC

Aluminium screw closures

Aluminium screw closures have almost entirely replaced corks on bottles for spirits and are making inroads into replacing wine corks on cheaper labels. While they do not allow wine to mature in the bottle, they do not taint it, are easy to open and close, and can be recycled in the same way as aluminium drinks cans.

It can be argued that aluminium closures, along with synthetic corks, are threatening the traditional cork oak forests of Spain and Portugal.

Aluminium closures are also used on bottles for medicines, fine toiletries and olive oil. They are easily crimped on to the neck of the bottle and a break-off ring will provide clear evidence of tampering. Unlike corks, they do not need a special opener.

Crown caps

Crown caps for beer bottles are stamped from sheet steel with a coating of plastic on the underside. The heavy-duty crimping process means that traditionally they have been only suitable for glass bottles. Recent developments in packaging have led to aluminium and PEN (a plastic compound) bottles, which are also sealed with crown caps.

The caps are easily recycled and can be separated from general waste with electromagnets.

Steel lids

Steel twist lids are widely used to seal glass jars. They are cheap, easily recycled and offer a good graphic surface. Pressed steel closures for (paint) tins and cardboard tubes are less common.

CLOSURES – PLASTIC

Flip-top/screw-top

Flip-top/screw-top closures for HDPE bottles tend to be made from PP, but some use HDPE and other plastics. A huge range of colours and finishes, including metallics and pearlescents, are available, which often makes it impractical to sort lids effectively for recycling, even though both HDPE and PP are recyclable.

Plastic pull-tops

Plastic pull-tops were originally introduced on detergent bottles and are now usually seen on bottles for drinks, especially water. They are used on bottles as small as 200 ml (a standard beverage can holds 330 ml), and normally comprise a screw closure, a pull spout (typically PP) and a clear overcap. The plastics are recyclable, but in practice are not always suitable for local authority collection.

Neat and convenient though the pull-tops are, the premise of using so much material for a single-use disposable product is questionable. A pull-top performs more or less the same function as a standard screw cap, but can contain three times as much plastic.

PUMPS/ATOMIZERS/ FOAMERS

Plastic pumps (typically made from PP) are commonly used for fragrances and toiletries, and also for less glamorous products, such as automotive degreasers and large catering-size containers for sauce. They are usually not recyclable, and would be more environmentally friendly if refills of their products could be made available.

Alternative packs for lotions and sauces that avoid using pumps might include plastic tubes (which are often not recyclable), doy bags and tottles (inverted HDPE bottles that rest on a wide PP cap).

Fragrance manufacturers have largely resisted environmental pressures, but a few have reverted to a modern take on the puffer-type atomizer. Perfumes also can be applied with a traditional dabber, which would be preferable to a pump atomizer.

Airless pumps (made from PP) often rely on expelling air from a straight-sided injection-moulded container. A shuttle at the base is pulled upwards to expel the product. This principle is often applied to toothpaste and various cosmetic lotions.

Another method is to pump air into a bottle containing bagged liquid, forcing the liquid out. This is more extravagant with materials than conventional pumps, but the product may be air-sensitive. As with most pumped products, there is usually a less wasteful alternative pack format, such as a bottle, doy bag or flexible tube.

Trigger tops have enabled the development of a wide variety of newer cleaning products. They contain several plastic parts (made from PP), a tube and a spring. They can potentially be reused with refill bottles, although in practice this option is not often offered by manufacturers.

In many ways this delivery system has inspired and driven product development, rather than the reverse. In particular, it has made foaming cleaners possible.

Trigger packs are especially wasteful and overdue for replacement by an alternative dispensing format. There is arguably little difference between spraying a cleaning product and wiping it with a cloth and applying it with a cloth straight from a standard bottle.

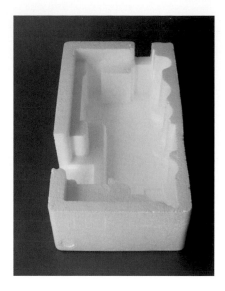

TRANSIT PACKAGING

Typical materials:

- **plastic** – XPS (polystyrene foam), LDPE (polyethylene foam), PP *(see pp. 150-60)*
- **hydrolytically degradable plastics** *(see p. 190)*
- **bioplastics** *(see p. 196 [paperfoam], p. 195 [starch], p. 197 [PLA, foamed])*
- **cardboard** *(see p. 174)*
- **recycled paper pulp** *(see p. 180)*

Transit packaging takes many forms and is usually comprised of a corrugated cardboard box with some sort of structural support to protect the product. Retail supply chains often use a system of reusable PP crates to distribute their products, which significantly reduces cardboard waste.

POLYSTYRENE FOAM OR EXPANDED POLYSTYRENE (XPS) TRANSIT PACKAGING

Polystyrene foam is an inexpensive and effective transit packaging material. It is lightweight, but difficulties in disposal and recycling, as well as its tendency to break up and blow into waterways, arguably outweigh the environmental gains this provides. It is still popular with manufacturers despite its poor environmental profile.

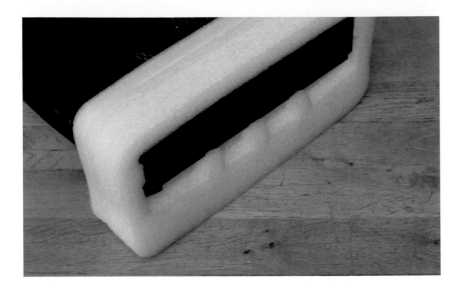

OTHER FOAM TRANSIT PACKAGING

Polyethylene foam (LDPE) is more expensive and denser, but more robust, than polystyrene foam. It does not break apart so easily and can potentially be reused. Recycling it is straightforward, but it is not usually collected.

There are biodegradable bioplastic alternatives to XPS foam, such as foamed potato starch pellets, which are hydrolytically degradable and therefore do not pose a threat to wildlife if discarded outdoors. Foamed PLA can be moulded in the same way as XPS foam, but is much more resistant to degradation than potato starch and emits methane in landfill.

CARDBOARD TRANSIT PACKAGING

Corrugated cardboard is an excellent support for many types of product, from televisions to mobile phones. It does not have the impact absorbency, mouldability or lightness of XPS foam, but benefits from high recycled content, recyclability and printability, which can help with the presentation of higher value products.

OTHER TYPES OF TRANSIT PACKAGING

Typical materials:

- **moulded pulp trays** *(see Trays, p. 216)*
- **bubble wrap**

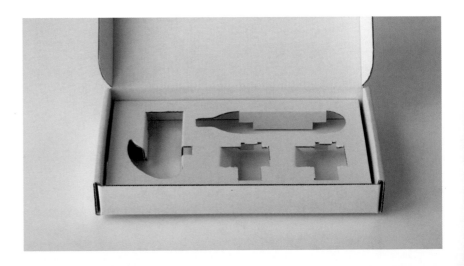

INKS

Most inks use petroleum-based solvents that aid print quality and improve their drying times, but they also release volatile organic compounds (VOCs) into the atmosphere during the drying process and they can potentially leach from landfill.

The migration of mineral oils from inks used in newspapers has recently been in the press. A Swiss study has shown that these petroleum-based oils, used as solvents to disperse pigment, can migrate from recycled card through barrier materials such as plastic bags and contaminate food products. Several manufacturers of breakfast cereals have stopped using recycled card in their packaging and other food manufacturers are trying to source newsprint-free recycled card.

Food scares are a rarity nowadays, which perhaps underscores how far packaging has come, so the link between contamination and recycled card could be a setback for the recycling industry. This is a major issue both for food producers, who need to ensure the safety of their product, and newspaper manufacturers, who need to find markets for their paper waste. Depending on the outcome of further research, legislation could be enacted to reduce the mineral-oil content in newspapers or to secure mineral-oil-free recycled card.

Soy- and vegetable-oil-based inks have recently become widely available. They contain significantly fewer VOCs, although a small amount of petroleum content is usually necessary to give realistic drying times. Soy inks tend to give a brighter image than conventional petroleum-based ones. They run on conventional presses, but can be more costly than conventional inks, particularly because soy and other vegetable oils, such as palm oil, are increasingly in demand for a wide range of applications.

Another alternative is to use UV inks, which dry rapidly under UV light. These are solid and do not contain VOCs, but they require specialist printing facilities, so are likely to be more costly than conventional inks. UV-cured inks cannot always be de-inked conventionally so are more difficult to recycle.

Electron beam (EB) inks, also VOC-free, are cured by being bombarded by electrons, as their name suggests. They are less costly and reactive than UV inks, but the EB hardware is expensive. Like UV inks they can present problems when they are repulped because de-inking is not always effective using conventional means.

Both EB and UV inks can cause skin irritations.

Water-based inks for flexo- and gravure printing do not contain VOCs, but are less straightforward to print. The equipment needs to be cleaned more often and the paper or card can curl. Additional heat is required for drying, which affects their environmental profile.

PRINT COATINGS/VARNISHES

Protective print coatings and varnishes tend to use the same processes as printing, so they fall into solvent-based, aqueous, UV and EB categories.

Holographic effects are usually achieved by incorporating a laminated layer of metallized polyester, which usually makes paperboard cartons non-recyclable by conventional means.

LIFE CYCLE ANALYSIS

The pressures for manufacturers and retailers to reach emissions targets and demonstrate environmental commitment to their customers has necessarily led to an evaluative approach to design so that any environmental benefits can be fully quantified.

At its most basic, manufacturers are able to make quick calculations about the material savings they have made. If, for instance, they reduce the amount of card used in a pack by 10 per cent they can quickly assess how much card, by weight, would be saved over the course of a year. Government targets are often based on making material reductions, and certainly landfill is usually taxed by weight, so these simple calculations can be extremely useful in making design judgements.

It may be necessary to work out the total energy usage, or greenhouse-gas emissions, particularly when comparing a range of designs and materials, rather than simply aiming to reduce materials.

LCA – life cycle assessment or life cycle analysis – is the process by which the amount of energy consumed in the manufacture, transportation and disposal of a given product can be measured to establish its effect on the environment.

Many different organizations use LCA to make comparative judgements on the day-to-day products we buy, as well as the processes used to make them. Retailers, such as Walmart, are increasingly demanding information about net energy or emissions consumption from their suppliers in their efforts to reduce their environmental impact.

To make a product life cycle analysis calculation a value is assigned to all the processes and materials in the life cycle, including gathering and processing raw materials, transportation to the manufacturing plant, manufacturing the product and packaging, transportation to the retailer, even the energy or emissions used in disposal or saved by recycling.

When looking at life cycle assessment figures it is important to know exactly what has been measured, as there are several different standards for methodology. The calculations for a packaging life cycle can only be approximations, because there are so many variables, such as the distance travelled to store, the amount of refrigeration, how far the product has to travel to be recycled, etc.

While the calculations can be extremely complex, a number of specialist computer programs can give approximate results, based on known values of materials, processes and methods of transportation. These can be extremely useful in making comparative judgements, but are no substitute for a full LCA from real-life data. The task for gathering LCA information is becoming simpler as more and more suppliers and manufacturers record their own data. For instance, manufacturers of materials usually give energy-consumption figures in their product specification sheets.

Deciding about which material(s) to use has to take into account the existing manufacturing set-up and the cost (both financial and environmental) of replacing it. This is another factor that makes lightweighting materials a popular environmental strategy, as it tends to have far fewer complications and environmental implications than adopting alternative packaging formats.

In an energy LCA each material can be represented in the form of energy/mass (for example, MJ/kg), based on the total amount of energy generated in mining, refining and processing it. By using these figures to calculate the energy/volume of capacity a direct comparison between materials can be made.

In the example from the Cambridge-MIT Institute the energy-efficiency of several materials in containing 1 litre of liquid was compared.

This demonstrates that steel is the most efficient material and glass and aluminium are the least, although recycled aluminium is 95 per cent more efficient than virgin aluminium (approximately 10 MJ/kg). Another factor with the potential to change the values of these materials is the reusability of glass bottles.

CARBON FOOTPRINTING

Carbon footprinting is an LCA format based purely on emissions of greenhouse gases at each stage of the life cycle. Even though they may include carbon dioxide, methane, nitrous oxide, etc., the results are typically expressed in grams of their carbon dioxide equivalent, as a point of reference.

CONTAINER TYPE	Glass	PE	PET	Aluminium	Steel
Mass (g)	325	38	25	20	45
Mass/Volume (g/litre)	433	38	62	45	102
Energy Mass (MJ/kg)	14	80	84	200	23
Energy/volume (MJ/litre)	8.2	3.2	5.4	9	2.4

There is no set methodology, so, although similar approaches are taken, some scientists urge caution in interpreting the results. For instance, not all greenhouse gases may be included in calculations (and not all are easily calculated), workers' journeys to their factory may be included or left out, and natural carbon dioxide emissions from land are often not included.

Carbon footprinting is becoming the method of choice for measuring the environmental impact of packaging and products. The Carbon Trust, for example, has a high-profile LCA labelling system. The label is a quick and easy way to compare products, helped by an engaging image which is easily translated into a logo. Some detractors criticize the image of a footprint, implying area, being linked to a measurement of weight. There is also some confusion over how a gas can be expressed as a weight. The weight is simply a measurement of what the individual molecules weigh.

Only a few retailers and manufacturers have published a carbon footprint for each of their products, and these can make for some interesting comparisons, as the entire product is footprinted, rather than just the packaging element. As carbon footprinting of individual products is still a novelty, companies that take the plunge and release data can expect to be put under intense scrutiny.

Innocent, a United Kingdom manufacturer of fruit smoothies, and Coca-Cola recently released carbon footprint information within a few weeks of each other and comparisons were immediately drawn between them. The comparisons were effectively between a corporate multinational producer of drinks from concentrate with massive resources and economies of scale and a national producer in the Ben & Jerry mould with a reputation for using fresh ingredients and behaving responsibly towards the environment, with a strictly ethical approach.

Coca-Cola was the clear winner, which prompted all sorts of implications of hypocrisy on the part of Innocent, who, while not being entirely blameless, make an entirely different type of product. Interestingly, Innocent's packaging emissions paled into insignificance against the emissions from manufacturing the product, whereas Coca-Cola's were a sizable proportion compared to making their product.

To a certain extent the story did no favours for carbon footprinting as a process, because most people in the United Kingdom are aware of Innocent's environmental and ethical aims, even if the company sometimes fall short of achieving them.

Carbon footprinting and carbon offsetting go hand in hand. Once the carbon footprint of a product, service, company, etc. has been established, carbon offsets can be bought to mitigate their effects on the environment. These take the form of investments in a wide range of environmental sustainability projects, such as wind farms, solar power, biomass boiler manufacturing, hydroelectric schemes and tree-planting initiatives. Much of the investment is voluntary, either by individuals or companies. Many companies see environmentally responsible retailing as a key part of what they offer, so eagerly advertise their contributions to carbon offsetting programmes.

Large manufacturers may have a cap set by government on the amount of emissions they create. These can be offset by buying tradable carbon credits. For instance, a manufacturer who exceeds their emissions output may buy credits from one operating within their allowance. Carbon offsetting schemes may contribute to generating carbon credits.

Carbon calculations are becoming an important metric of modern life; there are even websites devoted to working out personal carbon footprints. Carbon footprinting will almost inevitably become more of a feature in retailing, through legislation if not voluntarily.

ECOLOGICAL FOOTPRINTING

Another LCA method is to measure a product's effect on the earth's resources. Specifically the 'amount of biologically productive land and water area required to produce the resources consumed and assimilate the wastes generated'.

The results are measured in global hectares (GHA) or acres, and give a graphic and easily understood measurement of a product's impact on the planet. This method is particularly controversial among some traditional LCA, analysts claim it lacks scientific rigor.

Ecological footprinting is most often used to measure the environmental effect of businesses or households, rather than individual items, but it could well be applied to products in the same vein as carbon footprinting.

RECYCLING AND SUSTAINABILITY SYMBOLS

RECYCLING SYMBOLS AND ECO-LABELS ARE A SIMPLE WAY OF GIVING THE CONSUMER CONFIDENCE THAT A PRODUCT IS ENVIRONMENTALLY FRIENDLY. THEY FALL INTO TWO BROAD CATEGORIES: THE PURELY INFORMATIVE AND SYMBOLS THAT DEMONSTRATE SOME LEVEL OF ENVIRONMENTAL ATTAINMENT. THERE IS A GREAT DEAL OF COMPETITION TO CREATE CERTIFICATION SYSTEMS, AND ALL SYMBOLS ARE NOT EQUAL. SOME MANUFACTURERS HAVE CREATED THEIR OWN, WHICH CAN MISLEAD CONSUMERS INTO THINKING THEY HAVE BEEN AWARDED BY AN INDEPENDENT AUTHORITY (SEE '10 SIGNS OF GREENWASH', P. 131)

RETAIL GOODS

INFORMATION

Recyclable

Universally-recognized, catch-all symbol. 'Recyclable' does not necessarily mean 'widely recyclable', and whether packaging can be recycled depends on local recycling facilities.

Compostable (Europe)

Suitable for composting, depending on whether a local authority accepts packaging.

Green dot (Europe)

The manufacturer contributes to a packaging recovery system to comply with national recovery obligations. Sometimes misused as a generic recycling symbol.

The 'Recycle now' logo (United Kingdom)

Pack is easy to recycle. Gives much fuller information about packaging than the 're-cyclable symbol' and, based on UK averages, takes into account the likelihood of suitable recycling facilities being available locally.

ENVIRONMENTAL ATTAINMENT

European eco-label

Non-food products and services that conform to stringent environmental criteria aimed at reducing environmental impact throughout the life cycle of the product.

Nordic eco-label (Sweden, Norway, Denmark, Finland, Iceland)

Promotes sustainable consumerism. It denotes that the product has reached a high environmental standard.

Blue angel (Germany)

The first environmental award for retail goods, created in 1977 and still highly regarded.

Green seal (United States)

Goods and services have been independently life-cycle assessed, from raw materials to disposal, and the environmental impact has been minimized.

Green label (Thailand)

Multicategory environmental standard.

PAPER AND CARD

INFORMATION

RESY (on corrugated card)

The card can be recycled or reclaimed.

Totally chlorine free

Virgin paper made without using chlorine.

Processed chlorine free

Recycled paper reprocessed without using chlorine.

ENVIRONMENTAL ATTAINMENT

Programme for Endorsement of Forest Certification (worldwide)

Promotes production from environmentally and socially responsible forestry.

National Association of Paper Manufacturers (United Kingdom)

Guarantees 50 per cent, 75 per cent or 100 per cent recovered fibre, not including mill waste.

Sustainable Forestry Initiative (North America)

Environmental forestry standard for timber-based goods.

RECYCLING

PLASTICS

These international symbols are not a guarantee of recyclability. For instance, depending on location PET bottles may be collected for recycling, but PET blister packaging may not.

PET (Polyethylene teraphthalate)

Clear and tinted beverage and toiletry bottles, meal trays.

HDPE (High-density polyethylene)

Milk bottles, detergents, and toiletry packs.

METALS

PVC (Polyvinyl chloride)

Food trays, blister toiletry packs.

Recyclable steel

Commonly seen on food cans and aerosols.

LDPE (Low-density polyethylene)

Carrier bags, bin liners, bread bags, frozen food packs, bubble wrap, plastic lids for milk containers.

Recyclable aluminium

Drinks cans, aerosols, food trays etc.

PP (Polypropylene)

Food tubs, lids, trays for microwavable meals.

GLASS

PS (Polystyrene)

Yogurt pots, foam food trays, burger boxes, vending cups, protective transit packaging.

Recycle glass

A request rather than a description.

Any other plastics

RESOURCES

Environmental interest

www.treehugger.com

www.environmental-expert.com

www.greenerchoices.org

www.sustainableisgood.com

Packaging Interest

popsop.com

lovelypackage.com

Eco-labelling/law

www.ecolabelindex.com

www.packaginglaw.com

Environmentally friendly packaging info

www.wrap.org.uk

www.sustainablepackaging.org

www.incpen.org

Packaging museums

www.museumofbrands.com

www.verpackungsmuseum.de

INDEX

PICTURE CREDITS

2tr Photo: © Innocent Drinks Ltd, **2cl** Photo: Courtesy Ecolean AB, **2cc** Photo: Courtesy Dorset Cereals; Design: big fish design ltd, www.bigfish.co.uk, **2cr** Photo: Courtesy Sidel Group, **2bl** Photo: Courtesy Ecolean AB, **6** Photo: Thinkstock, **7tr** Photo: Thinkstock, **7b** Photo: ©iStockphoto.com / Tony Tremblay, **8, 9** Photo: Thinkstock, **11t** Photo: Courtesy Kenya Hara. Project Team: Client: Zen-noh (National Federation of Agricultural Co-operative Association) Iwafune; Creative director: Yoshikazu Banba; Art director/graphic designer: Kenya Hara, **11b** Photo: Courtesy Dorset Cereals; Design: big fish design ltd, www.bigfish.co.uk, **15c** © Jo St Mart, **15b, 21, 22r, 23, 25tl** Photo: Thinkstock, **25tr** Photo: BartlomiejMagierowski / Shutterstock.com, **25b** Photo: © iStockphoto.com / Sascha Burkard, **27** Photo: Thinkstock, **28, 29** Manufacturer Epicurean Europe Ltd. Structural design by Laurel Miller and Stephen Aldridge – a.m. associates. Graphics and branding by Ruth Tyson – Ark Design. Part of the South East Design "Sustainable Design and Innovation Project", project managed by Alison McFayden, **30-31, 32** Photo: Thinkstock, **35** Photo: © sylbohec / fotolia.com, 37, 43 Photo: Thinkstock, **45b** Photo: Courtesy Kraft Foods, **46** Courtesy Replenish, **47** Photo: Courtesy Tomra Systems ASA, **48** Photo: © Innocent Drinks Ltd, **49l** Photo: © Silviu G. Halmaghi / fotolia.com, 49 Photo: Thinkstock, **50l** Photo:

© Getty Images / Gamma-Rapho / Olivier Chouchana, **50r** Photo: © Getty Images / AFP, **51** Photo: © iStockphoto.com / jacus, **52** Photo: Courtesy Naya. Design owned by 'Naya Waters Inc.', developed by 'Bazooka Design', Montreal, QC, Canada, **53** Photo: © iStockphoto.com / Kieran Wills, **54r** Photo: Courtesy TerraCycle, **55** Photo: © azthesmudger / fotolia.com, 57t Photo: © iStockphoto.com / SimplyCreativePhotography, **57bl, 57br** Photo: Thinkstock, **58lt** © vincotte, **58r** Photo: © Daniel Rajszczak / Shutterstock.com, **59** Photo: ©iStockphoto.com / Richard Jemison, **61-63** Photo: Thinkstock, **65** Photo: Courtesy Sodastream UK, **67** Photo: © Irina Fischer / Shutterstock.com, **68l** © Jo St Mart, **69** Photo: Thinkstock, **71** Photo: © iStockphoto.com / Mike Clarke, **73** Photo: © iStockphoto.com / Zsolt Biczó, **80-85** Manufacturer Epicurean Europe Ltd. Structural design by Laurel Miller and Stephen Aldridge – a.m. associates. Graphics and branding by Ruth Tyson – Ark Design. Part of the South East Design "Sustainable Design and Innovation Project", project managed by Alison McFayden, **88** Photo: © Neiromobile / fotolia.com, 90 Photo: Courtesy Orangina, **91** Courtesy H.J. Heinz Company Limited, **92-93** Photo: Courtesy Kraft Foods, **95** Photo: © the food & drink innovation/pan macmillan, **96** Photo: Courtesy Hattomonkey. Hattomonkey created a packaging design for milk cocktail "From Joe". The design looks like a well-known hero. It is easy to create Batman's ears. Hattomonkey designers have created a brand new package form that look familiar and well-known since childhood, **97t** Photo: Thinkstock, **97b** Photo: © Innocent Drinks Ltd, **99** Courtesy Impulse, **104** Courtesy Tate + Lyle, **111, 112** Photo: Thinkstock, **113** Photo: Courtesy Kraft Foods, **119** Used with permission from McDonal's Restaurants Limited, **121** Photo: Courtesy Newton Running, **122** Photo: Pierre-Yves Babelon / Shutterstock.com, **123** Photo: Thinkstock, **125** Photo: Courtesy Kraft Foods, **129t** © green seal, **129c** © valpak, **132** Photo: Thinkstock, **136** Photo: © iStockphoto.com / Arthur Kwiatkowski, **137** Photo: © iStockphoto.com / Baris Arslan, **138-139** Help Remedies project: ChappsMalina – Product and Structural Design; Identity – Little Fury,

140-141 Photo: Courtesy Ecolean AB, **143** Courtesy Sidel Group, **144-145** Photo: Courtesy Sennheiser: Ms Sebnem Altug (Product Communication Manager Sennheiser), Projekt Kochstrasse Hannover (Pack Design Agency), **147** Courtesy Boots, **148-149** Photo: © Matthew Benoit / Shutterstock.com, **150** Photo: © iStockphoto.com / tasken, **152l** © stockexchange, **152r** Photo: © iStockphoto.com / Harald Richter, 153 Photo: Thinkstock, **154l** © stockexchange, **154r** Photo: © Alexey Stiop / fotolia.com, **155l** Photo: © iStockphoto.com / AdShooter, **156l** © stockexchange, **158l** © stockexchange, **158r** Photo: © Unclesam / fotolia.com, **159l** © stockexchange, **159r** Photo: © iStockphoto.com / Arturo M. Enriquez, **160l** Photo: © stockexchange, **160r** Photo: © iStockphoto.com / Jessica Morelli, **162** Photo: © ThKatz / fotolia.com, **163** Photo: © iStockphoto.com / Cody Johnson, **165, 166** Photo: Thinkstock, **167r** Photo: © Ingo Bartussek / fotolia.com, 168 Photo: © iStockphoto.com / luoman, **169tr** Photo: © Bruce Amos / Shutterstock.com, **169b** Photo: Courtesy Teisseire, **170** Photo: Thinkstock, **175** Photo: © Denis Pepin / fotolia.com, **178** Photo: © Moreno Soppelsa / Shutterstock.com, **181** Photo: © iStockphoto.com / Huguette Roe, **185** Photo: Thinkstock, **189** Photo: © Javier Tuana / Shutterstock.com, **190** Photo: © iStockphoto.com / Srebrina Yaneva, **195** Photo: © Gary L. / Shutterstock.com, **199** Photo: © iStockphoto.com / Karsten Bidstrup, **200** Photo: © iStockphoto.com / yungshu chao, **206** Photo: Thinkstock, **208r** Photo: © Martin Spurny / fotolia.com, 210r Photo: © iStockphoto.com / ALEAIMAGE, **211, 213r, 215r** Photo: Thinkstock, **221** Photo: © iStockphoto.com / Mark Wragg, **224l** Courtesy Goko, design by Laurel Miller and Stephen Aldridge – a.m. associates and Proworx, **228r, 229tl, 229tr** Photo: Thinkstock, **237lc2** © valpak, **237lb** © recyclenow, **237rt** © eu label, **237rc1** © Nordic Ecolabelling, **237rc2** © blue angel award, **237rc3** © green seal, **237rb** © green label thailand, **238lc1, 238lc2** © chlorinefreeproducts.org, **238lc3** © pefc, **238lb** © NAPM, **238rt** © sfiprogram.org, **238rb, 239l** © stockxchange

For Matthew, Robin and Anna

ACKNOWLEDGEMENTS

As structural packaging designers ourselves we know how important intelligent design is when creating great packaging. We would like to thank all the brilliant fellow packaging professionals who have contributed to this book. Special thanks go to the designers and companies who have contributed to the case studies for their help in submitting images and supplying information about their pieces of iconic packaging.

We would like to extend our thanks to Robert Opie at the Museum of Brands for allowing us to interview him and for his very special collection of historic packaging which is invaluable reference material for all packaging design professionals.

We extend our thanks to the team at Laurence King – especially Jo Lightfoot for commissioning this book and then being really, really patient. Also Donald Dinwiddle, Sue George and Anne Townley for their brilliant editing and production skills (and their patience), plus Jo St Mart for her stalwart help in image sourcing.

Laurel Miller and Stephen Aldridge